Advances in Educational Psychology 1

edited by W. D. Wall and V. P. Varma

Advances in Educational Psychology 1

 University of London Press Ltd.

ISBN 0 340 15463 2

University of London Press Ltd
St Paul's House, Warwick Lane, London EC4P 4AH

Printed and bound in Great Britain by
T. & A. Constable Ltd, Edinburgh EH7 4NF

Contents

Preface

This book has a double unity. It is a series of contributions from colleagues and former students of Professor Vernon aimed to mark their admiration of the man and his work. But it is more than a *festschrift*. The papers build into a coherent statement of advances in our knowledge, mainly but by no means exclusively, of the domains of intellectual ability and cognitive development—the area of study on which, more than any other, Vernon has left his mark.

Vernon himself neither neglected the interaction of personality variables with intelligence nor the dimensions of culture and environment as determinants of cognitive growth. The various chapters of this book follow his distinguished lead and discuss the whole range from birth to old age, consider the interaction of personality variables and intellect and discuss aspects of creativity.

The editors would like to thank the contributors, all of them exceptionally busy people, for the willingness and promptitude with which they responded to our request and accepted our general suggestions as to the topic on which they should write. We would like too to thank The British Psychological Society which has agreed to receive all royalties from the book and place them in a P. E. Vernon Fund.

W. D. Wall
V. P. Varma
1971

The contributors

H. J. Butcher
Professor of Educational Psychology, University of Sussex

Sheila M. Chown
Lecturer in Psychology, Bedford College, University of London

A. D. B. Clarke
Professor of Psychology, University of Hull

Ann M. Clarke
Research Fellow, Department of Psychology, University of Hull

W. A. de Silva
Lecturer in Education, Department of Education, University of Ceylon

H. J. Eysenck
Professor of Psychology, University of London; Director of the Psychological Laboratories, Institute of Psychiatry and Psychologist to the Maudsley and Bethlem Royal Hospitals

L. S. Hearnshaw
Professor of Psychology, University of Liverpool

J. Kane
Senior Lecturer in Physical Education, St Mary's College of Education, University of London Institute of Education

K. Lovell
Professor of Educational Psychology, University of Leeds

E. A. Peel
Professor of Education (Educational Psychology Division), University of Birmingham

R. W. Pickford
Professor of Psychology, University of Glasgow

W. D. Wall
Dean of the University of London Institute of Education

S. Wiseman
Formerly Director of the National Foundation for Educational Research

V. P. Varma
Educational Psychologist, London Borough of Brent Child Guidance Service

Philip Vernon

This volume displays in a limited but varied series of ways the influence which Philip Vernon has exerted and continues to exert on his contemporaries and upon the course of research in educational psychology. His career too illustrates, as it has contributed to, what I might call the second great expansion of knowledge about children and the processes of education. His masters were men like Myers, Spearman, Burt, Stout, McDougall, McK. Cattell, Rivers and, above all, first F. C. Bartlett and then Gordon Allport. His father, H. M. Vernon, was the pioneer of industrial psychology in Britain during the 1914-18 war and afterwards. His students first at Jordanhill and Glasgow University, and then—from 1949-68 —at the Institute of Education, London, have carried on and developed the tradition he established of minute analysis and cautious synthesis of the literature as a prelude to well designed and exact studies. He has not perhaps been, at least until recently, an innovator in the sense that Burt has but from the outset of his career he has been expressing views (backed by evidence) on a wide range of topics—musical perception, personality testing, multiple choice testing, factor analysis and the nature of intelligence. More than anything else he has set a tradition of rigour and scholarship in educational psychology while at the same time attacking real and burning problems of actuality within his strict methodology. He has never been a populariser but the very practical nature of the problems to which his attention has been turned makes his name well known to those concerned with the day to day business of education.

Vernon was born in 1905 of a medical family on his father's side; his mother was a historian with strong interests in music and Italian art. He was the only boy in a family of four and in some respects rather solitary both by nature and circumstances. His childhood interests, though varied, were practical and in the main biological. He began learning the piano quite early and throughout his life his musical interests have been wide. Indeed so marked were his musical abilities and tastes that he was sent for four months to Vienna after leaving school, partly to learn German but mainly to study music. On his return, while his parents were willing to allow him to follow a professional musical career, he agreed that this would be hazardous and read chemistry, physiology and physics, gaining his First in Natural Sciences at Cambridge after two years.

It so happened that his college was St John's, where McDougall, Cattell,

Burt, Rivers, F. C. Bartlett and others had worked, and where Udny Yule was one of his tutors. Encouraged by this and by his father who regarded psychology as the subject of the future, he switched to psychology in his third year. He gained a First, a research studentship, and embarked on a Ph.D. Not unexpectedly his field of study was the psychology of music, but he read widely in psychometrics, industrial psychology and personality theory, constructed a group test of intelligence for university students and older secondary public school pupils, and carried out a study of the socio-psychological aspects of rowing—the one sport which he had energetically practised at school and university.

After a period as psychologist to the London County Council (at Maudsley Bartlett encouraged his bright young student, even though Vernon's tastes and interests went markedly outside those traditional to the Cambridge department, and in 1929 helped him to gain a fellowship to the USA. There he worked for a year with Mark May on personality testing and spent a further year at Harvard under Gordon Allport. He carried out, as part of his work at Yale, an elaborate study of the then existing personality tests, in connection with the final stages of the Character Education Enquiry; at Harvard he worked on the Allport-Vernon Study of Values and the Studies of Expressive Movement.

After a period as psychologist to the London County Council (at Maudsley Hospital) he was appointed to the headship of the Department of Psychology in Jordanhill in 1935. He wrote his first book, The Measurement of Abilities, and turned his attention increasingly to psychometric studies of examinations, intelligence and attainment. He married in 1937.

As for a number of his contemporaries, the period from 1940 to the end of the war was a formative one contributing to a change in direction. He became a 'back room boy' concerned with personnel selection in the Army and the Navy. Over the four or more years of his service, he produced on the average one report, comparable to a journal article, a week! His musical interests lapsed because of his intense activity, but writing of this, he says, perceptively:

'I did not really miss it, since calculating innumerable correlations, factor and regression analyses (without a computer), filled very much the same functions in my make-up. I am not a trained statistician, but I would claim to be rather adept in comprehending and interpreting the implications of sets of figures, in much the same way as I have been able, since the age of 16, to analyse and distinguish the underlying patterns and relations of notes in orchestral and other music. A centroid factor analysis, a Bach fugue, a Gothic cathedral, all yield a similar aesthetic excitement. Hence, although I still play the piano (especially two-piano music with my wife), and enjoy occasional concerts and L.P. records, I no longer have the same persisting need for music; and this need, it would seem, has to some extent determined the psychometric bias of my psychological interests.'

He returned briefly to Glasgow after the war, but his attachment to applied psychological work led him back (after the death of his first wife and his second *marriage) to the Senior Psychologist's Department in the Admiralty. The cautious anonymity of the peace-time Civil Service proved however much less satisfying than the excitements of war-time personnel selection. In 1949 he succeeded Hamley in the Chair of Educational Psychology at the Institute of Education, University of London.*

This proved a highly creative stimulus. He published three books arising largely out of his war-time work, gained the D.Sc. of London University, became President of Section J of the British Association, President of the British Psychological Society and made a great many lecture tours covering in all twenty-eight countries.

Perhaps as a consequence of this change of job, perhaps because of simple maturation, the nature of his work changed. Up till 1950 most of his publications had been valuable critical syntheses of the work of others and contributions to methodology—both of a very high order. Increasingly since then he has become, to quote his own words: '. . . . concerned with the human implications of my psychometric approach. Educational and social issues are far too complex to be settled by tests and statistics—for example the controversies over the 11+ and comprehensivisation—yet psychologists and sociologists, in virtue of their scientific training and research findings, can provide many relevant facts and perhaps reason a little more logically than the politician, parent or school teacher.'

He spent, in 1957 and again in 1961-62, lengthy periods in America where he wrote his Personality Assessment—a Critical Survey. *On his return in 1962 the Institute of Education generously freed him from the administrative duties of head of the Department of Educational Psychology and enabled him to devote himself full time to research and advanced teaching.*

A number of challenges offered themselves at this time. He was invited in 1960 to advise the Ministries of Education of Jamaica and Trinidad on their problems of secondary selection. 'I thrived', he writes, 'on the challenge of adjusting my Western ideas to a totally new setting, of overcoming the barriers of race and eliciting the information and opinions of local educationists and civil servants, as well as those of expatriates. From these enquiries, and from observation and testing in schools, one realised only too clearly the effects of primitive conditions of up-bringing, extreme poverty, linguistic handicap, poor teaching, and of the financial and other difficulties of a developing country, on intellectual development.'

Later in 1963, with the financial support of the Association for the Aid of Crippled Children in New York, he was able to embark on the extended series of cross-cultural conditions that retard mental development. He and his wife tested, with a wide range of individual and group tests, samples of boys in England, the Hebrides, Jamaica, Alberta (Canadian Indians), the Canadian

Arctic (Eskimos), Tanzania and Uganda, studying their cultural, home and educational backgrounds.

These researches, which extended over three or more years, were analysed and written up in 1969 and published as Intelligence and Cultural Environment. *This is, for Philip Vernon, an unusual book in that, as well as the usual meticulous weighing and presentation of evidence, it contributes to discussion on the social, political and educational causes of backwardness. It stands as a model of the integration of a careful scientific approach with a genuine sympathy for human problems.*

Throughout this period, Vernon accepted responsibility for large numbers of advanced students whom he tutored for their M.A. and Ph.D. degrees of the University of London. These men and women staff the educational services in Great Britain and the Commonwealth; they have made and are making an immense contribution to the work of education. More even than in his books, Vernon's influence, scholarly, meticulous, scientific and humane, is exerted through them.

In 1968, he decided to forsake the rigours of the English climate, both natural and economic, for a senior post in the University of Calgary in Canada. Here with rather more time he is continuing to pursue his researches into the factors that promote or retard the growth of abilities and character—the theme which has dominated his work throughout his life and to which he has made a contribution second to none.

W. D. Wall, London 1971

Bibliography of Vernon's published work up to 1971

BOOKS AND MAJOR REPORTS

(With G. W. ALLPORT) *Studies in Expressive Movement.* London: Macmillan 1933.

The Assessment of Personal Qualities by Verbal Methods. Industrial Health Research Board Report, No. 83, 1938.

The Measurement of Abilities. London: University of London Press, 1940.

The Measurement of Abilities. 2nd rev. edit. London: University of London Press, 1956.

The Training and Teaching of Adult Workers. London: University of London Press, 1942.

(With J. B. PARRY) *Personnel Selection in the British Forces.* London: University of London Press, 1947.

The Structure of Human Abilities. London: Methuen, 1950.

La Structure des Aptitudes Humaines. French translation by M. N. Reuchlin. Paris: Presses Universitaires de France, 1952. Second English edition, with Supplement. London: Methuen, 1961.

Personality Tests and Assessments. London: Methuen, 1953.

(With C. A. MACE, eds.) *Current Trends in British Psychology.* London: Methuen, 1953.

Secondary School Selection (ed.). London: Methuen, 1957.

Educational Testing and Test Form Factors. Princeton, N.J.: Educational Testing Service, Report RB-58-3, 1958.

Intelligence and Attainment Tests. London: University of London Press, 1960. Spanish translation, Buenos Aires: Victor Leru, 1962.

Selection for Secondary Education in Jamaica. Kingston, Jamaica: Government Printer, 1961.

Personality Assessment: A Critical Appraisal. London: Methuen, 1964.

Selection to Secondary Schools in Tanzania. London: Ministry for Overseas Development (cyclostyled), 1966.

Intelligence and Cultural Environment. London: Methuen, 1969.

TESTS

(With G. W. ALLPORT) *The Study of Values*. Boston: Houghton Mifflin, 1931.

(With G. W. ALLPORT and G. LINDZEY) *The Study of Values*. 2nd edition. Boston: Houghton Mifflin, 1951.

The Standardisation of a Graded Word Reading Test. Publications of the Scottish Council for Research in Education, No. XII. London: University of London Press, 1938.

Graded Arithmetic-Mathematics Test. London: University of London Press, 1949.

Graded Arithmetic-Mathematics Test. Decimal Currency edition. London: University of London Press, 1971.

ARTICLES

'The psychology of rowing.' *Br. J. Psychol.*, 1928, **18**, 317-31.

'Non-musical factors in the appreciation of music.' *Musical Times*, 1929, pp. 123-4, 227-8, 320-1.

'Tests of temperament and personality.' *Br. J. Psychol.*, 1929, **20**, 97-117.

'The personality of the composer.' *Music and Letters*, 1930, **11**, 58-70.

'Method in musical psychology.' *Am. J. Psychol.*, 1930, **42**, 127-34.

'Synaesthesia in music.' *Psyche*, 1930, **10**, 22-40.

The phenomena of attention and visualization in the psychology of musical appreciation. *Br. J. Psychol.*, 1930, **21**, 50-63.

'A method for measuring musical taste.' *J. Appl. Psychol.*, 1930, **14**, 355-62.

(With G. W. ALLPORT) 'The field of personality.' *Psychol. Bull.*, 1930, **27**, 677-730.

(With G. W. ALLPORT) 'A test for personal values.' *J. abnorm. soc. Psychol.*, 1932, **26**, 231-48.

'Human temperament: the development of methods for assessing it.' *Eugen. Rev.*, 1932, **23**, 325-31.

'Some characteristics of the good judge of personality.' *J. soc. Psychol.*, 1933, **4**, 42-58.

'The apprehension and cognition of music.' *Proc. Mus. Assoc.*, 1933, **59**, 61-84.

'The American *vs.* the German methods of approach to the study of temperament and personality.' *Br. J. Psychol.*, 1933, **24**, 156-77.

'The Rorschach Inkblot Test.' *Br. J. med. Psychol.*, 1933, **13**, 89-118; 179-205; 271-95.

'The biosocial nature of the personality trait.' *Psychol. Rev.*, 1933, **40**, 533-48.

'The measurement of personality and temperament.' *Human Factor.*, 1934, **8**, 87-95.

'The attitude of the subject in personality testing.' *J. appl. Psychol.*, 1934, **18**, 165-77.

'Bodily chemistry and temperament.' *Med. Press and Circular*, 1934, **189**, 173-6.

'A new instrument for recording handwriting pressure.' *Br. J. educ. Psychol.*, 1934, **4**, 310-16.

'Auditory perception. I. The Gestalt approach. II. The biological approach.' *Br. J. Psychol.*, 1934-5, **25**, 123-39; 265-83.

'Tests of temperament and character.' *The 1935 Yearbook of Education*, 509-27.

'Tests in aesthetics.' *The 1935 Yearbook of Education*, 528-36. Republished in *The Testing of Intelligence* (ed. H. R. Hamley). London: Evans, 1935.

'Can the total personality be studied objectively?' *Character Person.*, 1935, **4**, 1-10.

'Recent work on the Rorschach test.' *J. ment. Sci.*, 1935, **81**, 1-27.

'The significance of the Rorschach test.' *Br. J. med. Psychol.*, 1935, **15**, 199-217.

'The matching method applied to investigations of personality.' *Psychol. Bull.*, 1936, **33**, 149-77.

'The evaluation of the matching method.' *J. educ. Psychol.*, 1936, **27**, 1-17.

'A note on the standard error in the contingency matching technique.' *J. educ. Psychol.*, 1936, **27**, 704-9.

'A study of the norms and the validity of certain mental tests at a child guidance clinic.' *Br. J. educ. Psychol.*, 1937, **7**, 72-88; 115-37.

'The Stanford-Binet test as a psychometric method.' *Character Person.*, 1937, **6**, 99-113.

'The revised Stanford-Binet test.' *The 1938 Yearbook of Education*, 27-34.

'Intelligence test sophistication.' *Br. J. educ. Psychol.*, 1938, **8**, 237-44.

'Educational abilities of training college students.' *Br. J. educ. Psychol.*, 1939, **9**, 233-50.

'Questionnaires, attitude tests and rating scales.' *The Study of Society* (eds. F. C. Bartlett and E. J. Lindgren). London: Kegan Paul, 1939, pp. 199-229.

(With R. L. MORRISON) 'A new method of marking English compositions.' *Br. J. educ. Psychol.*, 1941, **11**, 109-19.

'An analysis of the conception of morale.' *Character Person.*, 1941, **9**, 283-94.

'Short tests of low-grade intelligence.' *Occup. Psychol.*, 1941, **15**, 107-11, 129-31.

'Psychological effects of air-raids.' *J. abnorm. soc. Psychol.*, 1941, **36**, 457-76.

'Is the doctrine of instincts dead? Some objections to the theory of human instincts.' *Br. J. educ. Psychol.*, 1942, **12**, 1-9.

'A study of war attitudes.' *Br. J. med. Psychol.*, 1942, **19**, 271-91.

'An experiment on the value of the film and filmstrip in the instruction of adults.' *Br. J. educ. Psychol.*, 1946, **16**, 149-62.

'Statistical methods in the selection of Army and Navy personnel.' *Suppl. to Jl. Ry. statist. Soc.*, 1946, **8**, 139-53.

(With M. MCKINLAY) 'Effects of vitamin and hormone treatment on senile patients.' *J. neurol. neurosurg. Psychiat.*, 1946, **9**, 87-92.

'Psychological tests in the Royal Navy, Army and A.T.S.' *Occup. Psychol.*, 1947, **21**, 53-74.

'The variations of intelligence with occupation, age and locality.' *Br. J. Psychol. statist. sec.*, 1947, **1**, 52-63.

'Research on personnel selection in the Royal Navy and the British Army.' *Am. Psychol.*, 1947, **2**, 35-51.

'A preliminary investigation of the vocabulary of Scottish children entering school. Word counts of infant readers.' *Studies in Reading*, Vol. 1. Scottish Council for Research in Education. London: University of London Press, 1948, pp. 93-171.

'Indices of item consistency and validity.' *Br. J. Psychol. statist. sec.*, 1948, **1**, 152-66.

'Occupational norms for the 20-minute progressive matrices test.' *Occup. Psychol.*, 1949, **23**, 48-9.

'The structure of practical abilities.' *Occup. Psychol.*, 1949, **23**, 81-96.

'Classifying highgrade occupational interests.' *J. abnorm. soc. Psychol.*, 1949, **44**, 85-96.

'The validation of Civil Service selection board procedures.' *Occup. Psychol.*, 1950, **24**, 75-95.

'Psychological studies of the mental quality of the population.' *Br. J. educ. psychol.*, 1950, **20**, 35-42.

'The estimation of difficulty of vocabulary.' *Br. J. educ. Psychol.*, 1950, **20**, 77-82.

'Post-graduate training of teachers in psychology.' *Br. J. educ. Psychol.*, 1950, **20**, 149-52.

'An investigation into post-war reading ability.' Appendix to: *Reading Ability*. Ministry of Education Pamphlet No. 18. HMSO, 1950.

'An application of factorial analysis to the study of test items.' *Br. J. Psychol. statist. sec.*, 1950, **3**, 1-15.

'The intelligibility of broadcast talks.' *B.B.C. Quarterly*, 1951, **5**, 206-12.

'Recent investigations of intelligence and its measurement.' *Eugen. Rev.*, 1951, **43**, 125-37.

'Intelligence tests.' *Times educ. Suppl.*, 1952.

'L'interprétation des testes d'intelligence.' *Travail. hum.*, 1952, **15**, 177-184.

'The assessment of personality.' *Advmt. Sci.*, 1952, **9**, 207-18.

'The psychological traits of teachers.' *The 1953 Yearbook of Education*, pp. 51-75.

'Practice and coaching effects in intelligence tests.' *Forum of Educ.*, 1954, **18**.

'Symposium on the effects of coaching and practice in intelligence tests.' V. Conclusions. *Br. J. educ. Psychol.*, 1954, **24**.

'How to use the I.Q. in counselling.' *J. nat. Assoc. of Deans of Women*, 1940, **4**, No. 1, 18-24.

'The individuality of keys.' *Musical Times*, 1942, pp. 105-7, 138-9.

'Recent developments in the measurement of intelligence and special abilities.' *Br. med. Bull.*, 1949, **6**, No. 1, 21-3.

'Modern educational psychology as a science.' *Univ. London Inst. Educ. Stud. in Educ.*, 1950, **1**.

'Educational Psychology.' *Encyclopaedia Britannica*, 1963, **7**, 1025-8.

(With G. D. MILLICAN) 'A further study of the reliability of English Essays.' *Br. J. statist. Psychol.*, 1954, **7**, 65-74.

'Use of intelligence tests in population studies.' *Eugen. Quart.*, 1954, **1**, 221-4.

'The psychology of intelligence and G.' *Q. Bull. Br. psychol. Soc.*, 1955, **26**, 1-14.

'Psychological testing.' *Chambers's Encyclopaedia*, 1950, **11**, 300-3. London: Newnes.

'The assessment of children.' *Univ. London Inst. Educ. Stud. in Educ.*, 1955, **7**, 189-215. London: Evans.

(With M. B. O'GORMAN and A. MCLELLAN) 'A comparative study of educational attainments in England and Scotland.' *Br. J. educ. Psychol.*, 1955, **25**, 195-203.

(With J. A. M. BROOKS) 'A study of children's interests and comprehension at a science museum.' *Br. J. Psychol.*, 1956, **47**, 175-82.

'Intelligence and intellectual stimulation during adolescence.' *Indian Psychol. Bull.*, 1957, **2**, 1-6.

'Secondary school education and selection in England.' *Educ. Forum*, 1957, **21**, 261-9.

'Critical notice: psychological tests and personnel decisions, by L. J. Cronback.' *Br. J. educ. Psychol.*, 1958, **28**, 80-3.

'Education and the psychology of individual differences.' *Harv. Educ. Rev.*, 1958, **28**, 91-104.

'A new look at intelligence testing.' *Educ. Res.*, 1958, **1**, 1-12.

'The relation of intelligence to educational backwardness.' *Educ. Rev.*, 1958, **11**, 7-15.

'Race and intelligence.' *New Scientist*, 1959, **5**, 170-1. Also in *Eugen. Rev.*, 1959, **51**, 99-101.

'The assessment of higher intellectual capacities.' *Pedgogisk Forskning*, 1959, Nos. 2 and 3.

'L'appréciation des qualités intellectuelles Supérieures.' *Travail hum.*, 1959, Nos. 1-2, 1-10.

'La selection dans les écoles secondaires d'Angleterre.' *Travail hum.*, 1959, Nos. 1-2, 233-8.

'Trends in secondary selection.' *Times Educ. Suppl.*, 1959, March 13th and 20th.

'The segregation of slow-learning children.' *Aust. J. Educ. of Backward Children*, 1960, **7**, 1-6.

The Contribution of Studies of Secondary School Selection to the Science of Mental Testing. Godfrey Thomson Lecture. Edinburgh: Moray House, 1960.

'The classification of abilities.' *Educ. Res.*, 1960, **2**, 184-93.

'Intellectual development in non-technological societies.' *Proc. XIV Congr. Appl. Psychol.* Copenhagen: Munksgaard, 1961, 94-105.

'The contributions to education of Sir Godfrey Thomson.' *Br. J. educ. Stud.*, 1962, **10**, 123-37.

'The determinants of reading comprehension.' *Educ. psychol. Measur.*, 1962, **22**, 269-86.

'Measurement of abilities, attitudes and personality traits.' In *Society: Problems and Methods of Study* (eds. A. T. Welford *et al.*). London: Routledge & Kegan Paul, 1962, 61-75.

'The pool of ability.' *Sociol. Rev. Monogr.*, 1963, No. 7, 45-57.

(With G. W. S. MACKAY) 'The measurement of learning ability.' *Br. J. educ. Psychol.*, 1963, **33**, 177-86.

An Introduction to Objective-Type Examinations. London: H.M.S.O. Examinations Bulletin No. 4.

'Creativity and intelligence.' *Educ. Res.*, 1964, **6**, 163-9.

(With K. RAY CHOWDHURY) 'An experimental study of imagery and its relation to abilities and interests.' *Br. J. Psychol.*, 1964, **55**, 355-364.

'Environmental handicaps and intellectual development.' *Br. J. educ. Psychol.*, 1965, **35**, 9-20, 117-26.

'Abilities and attainments in the Western Isles.' *Scot. Educ. J.*, 1965, **48**, 948-50.

'The criterion problem in selection and guidance.' *Occup. Psychol.*, 1965, **39**, 93-7.

'Evaluation objective des Résultats obtenus dans les Études de Niveau elevé.' *Travail hum.*, 1965, 203-12.

'Ability factors and environmental influences' (Walter Vandyke Bingham Lecture). *Am. Psychol.*, 1965, **20**, 723-33.

'Clinical and psychometric approaches to personality assessment in vocational counselling.' *Pedagogisk Forskning.* Oslo, 1965, 37-53.

'The personality system.' In *Studies in Psychology Presented to Cyril Burt* (eds. C. Banks and P. L. Broadhurst). London: University of London Press, 1965, 55-64.

'Educational and intellectual development among Canadian Indians and Eskimos.' *Educ. Rev.*, 1966, **18**, 79-91, 186-95.

'Development of current ideas about intelligence tests.' In *Genetic and Environmental Factors in Human Ability* (eds. J. E. Meade and A. S. Parkes). Edinburgh: Oliver & Boyd, 1966, 3-14.

'Modernos puntos de vista de la intelligencia.' Lima: Univ. de San Marcos, *Estudios Psicopedagogicos*, 1966, No. 10.

'Factors ambientales y desarrollo intellectual.' Quito: Univ. Central. *Publicaciones del Departamento de Orientation Professional*, 1966.

'A cross-cultural study of "creativity tests" with 11-year-old boys.' *New Res. in Educ.*, 1966, **1**, 135-46.

'Administration of group intelligence tests to East African pupils.' *Br. J. educ. Psychol.*, 1967, **37**, 282-91.

'Orientacion y seleccion para el ingreso a universidads.' Lima: Univ. de San Marcos, *Estudios Psicopedagogicos*, 1967, No. 11.

'Abilities and educational attainments in an East African environment.' *J. Spec. Educ.*, 1967, **4**, 335-45.

'Psychological studies of creativity.' *J. Child Psychol. Psychiat.*, 1967, **8**, 153-64.

'Measurements of learning.' In *Malnutrition, Learning and Behaviour* (ed. N. S. Scrimshaw). Cambridge, Mass: M.I.T. Press, 1968.

'What is potential ability?' (fifth C. S. Myers Lecture). *Bull. Br. psychol. Soc.*, 1968, **21**, No. 73, 211-19.

'Types of examinations.' *Yrbk. of Educ.*, 1969.

L. S. Hearnshaw

The concepts of aptitude and capacity*

The birth of differential psychology during the latter half of the nineteenth century was the outcome partly of developments in the biological sciences, and partly of practical demands in education, occupational life, and medicine. It was the result of forces impinging upon psychology from without, rather than a natural development from within psychology itself. Galton, who can be regarded as the founder of differential psychology, at any rate in its quantitative forms, worked with a very sketchy framework of general psychological theory, and to this day the concepts of aptitude and capacity, among the principal concepts of differential psychology, are imperfectly integrated with general psychology. The Canadian psychologist, G. A. Ferguson (1954),† observed a few years ago, 'at present no systematic theory, capable of generating fruitful hypotheses about behaviour, lies behind the study of human ability' (1). Contrariwise, in the principal systems of psychological theory (behaviourism, psychoanalysis, Gestalt theory) there is no obvious and integral place for the concepts of aptitude and capacity. The attempts of factor analysts on the one hand, and personalists (Stern, Allport and their followers) on the other have not as yet been sufficiently cogent to rectify the situation.

Three principal strands have gone to the making of modern psychology. First there is the Aristotelian strand, with its medieval and modern derivates, scholasticism and faculty psychology: secondly there is the empirical strand, deriving from the empirical philosophers of the seventeenth and eighteenth centuries: thirdly, there is the biological strand, a nineteenth century addition depending on discoveries and advances in neurophysiology, anatomy, evolutionary biology and genetics, medicine and psychiatry. Perhaps in the twentieth century we can add a fourth strand, the influence of the social sciences.

* A revised and extended version of a paper originally delivered at XII *Congrès International d'Histoire des Sciences* in Paris, August 1968.
† All references are given on pages 166 ff. References for this paper are arranged by number, but for the other papers they are in alphabetical order of author.

The concepts of aptitude and capacity are basically Aristotelian in origin. Aristotle analysed existence into four principal components (ἀρχαί), two static, matter and form, and two dynamic, potentiality and actuality (δύναμις and ἐνέργεια). All things have a fixed constitutive nature, and viewed *sub specie aeternitatis* the perfect precedes the imperfect, the whole the part, the realised the possible. The final perfection (ἐντελέχεια) is the essential being (τὸ τί ἦν εἶναι) of things. These concepts were applied by Aristotle to human nature in his treatises on psychology and ethics. In the soul Aristotle distinguished various potentialities—some active (δύναμις ποιητική), some passive (δύναμις παθητική)—some orectic, some rational. In the course of growth and activity these potentialities were developed into acquired dispositions (ἕξεις), moral and intellectual. The perfect man was the man whose potentialities had most fully attained in their expression (ἐνέργεια) the ideal of rationality, for man in his realised perfection (ἐντελέχεια) was a being acting according to his essence, which was reason (λόγος).

Aristotle's psychology was a coherent theoretical structure, derived from and hence concordant with his general metaphysical system. A central concept in this system was the concept of potentiality. The power of Aristotelianism was such that, in spite of the protests of certain Renaissance and modern thinkers, it has largely shaped the language of psychology, and until very recently European man's popular conceptions of human nature. The concepts of 'faculty', 'aptitude', 'ability', and 'capacity' are a residue of Aristotelianism.

The philosophy of the Greeks was adopted by the Romans, and its terminology translated into Latin. Aristotle's potentialities or powers (δυνάμεις) became the faculties (*facultates*) of Cicero. '*Facultates sunt, aut quibus facilius fit, aut sine quibus aliquid confici non potest*' (2). The Greek power of understanding (διανόια) became in Latin '*intelligentia*'. '*Intelligentia est, per quam animus ea perspicit quae sunt*' (3). The medieval scholastics adopted, refined and extended the apparatus and terminology of ancient philosophy. In Aquinas's subtle discussion of the powers (*potentiae animae*) of the soul (4) the essential unity of the soul is held to be compatible with a plurality of powers, provided that these powers are conceived as organised. 'Since the soul is one, and the powers are many . . . there must be some order among the powers of the soul' (5). Here we see the germs of that hierarchical conception of the soul's powers which was to influence Spearman and through him contemporary factor analysts. To the question whether intelligence is a power distinct from intellect Aquinas replies that 'Intelligence properly signifies the intellect's very act, which is to understand' (6). Moreover, because in man the intellect is united to a material body 'the individuality of the intelligent being' is a result.

The terminology of scholasticism, since the clerics were the school-masters of the Middle Ages, became incorporated into the vernaculars of Europe. 'Faculty', 'ability', 'capacity', and later 'aptitude' became every-day terms (*faculté, vermögen, capacité, fähigkeit, abilità*, etc.). In the fourteenth century Chaucer was speaking of abilities: 'I have perceived well by certaine evidences thine abilite to lerne science' (7). Two centuries later Shakespeare made mention of 'all our abilities, gifts, natures, shapes' (8).

Faculty psychology was the explicit and systematic expression of these ideas. Originally faculties were powers distinguished, as the scholas-tics had it, *per actus et objecta.* Faculty psychology was not merely a scheme of classification; though it was this, it was also an explanatory system. This system lost ground after the Galilean revolution, but in the eighteenth and early nineteenth centuries it 'revived' in the faculty psychology of Wolff in Germany, of Reid and Stewart in Scotland, and of Collard and Cousin in France. The primary divisions between the cog-nitive and the conative, between the sensuous and the rational, drawn by the scholastics were accepted by the faculty psychologists and formed the basis of the distinction between intellectual and active powers, and the foundation of the subsequent more detailed analysis within these major categories. With Sir William Hamilton, one of the most learned of the Scottish school who died in 1856, we find that an important criterion for the distinction of one faculty from another is that 'the two faculties are possessed by different individuals in very different degrees' (9). Memory and intelligence for instance are separate faculties, Hamilton notes, because some intelligent individuals have poor memories and vice versa (10). Faculty is clearly making a transition to a quantifiably assessable ability. Faculty psychology, in principle if not in detail, could have provided a theoretical framework for the concepts of aptitude and capacity, integrated with a main body of psychological theory. Meanwhile, however, faculty psychology had come under attack and the movements making for the development of scientific psychology in the nineteenth century were generally antagonistic to the faculty concept.

The reaction against faculties was a facet of the general seventeenth century revolt against Aristotle, 'who corrupted natural philosophy with his logic' (11) as Francis Bacon put it. This revolt involved above all the overthrow of the Aristotelian doctrine of final causation. 'A final cause', wrote Hobbes, 'has no place but in such things as have sense and will, and that also I shall prove hereafter to be an efficient cause' (12). Hobbes en-deavoured to assimilate the study of the human mind to the emerging world view of the physical sciences, and though his empirical successors did not always show his uncompromising consistency, the main burden of the empirical philosophy involved a denigration of faculties, a denial of innate capacities, and an emphasis on the adventitious nature of individual differences. The mind of Locke could be compared initially to 'white paper, void of all characters' (13). Explanation in faculty terms was a meaningless type of explanation. 'We may as properly say that the singing faculty sings, and the dancing faculty dances, as that the will chooses or that the understanding conceives, or, as is usual, that the will directs the understanding, or the understanding obeys, or obeys not, the will . . . It has misled many into a confused notion of so many distinct agents in us' (14).

Locke himself was a far from consistent thinker: he was critical of 'faculties', but spoke freely of 'powers'. Nevertheless the differences 'in the manners and abilities of men' were the result mainly of education and upbringing. In Locke's empiricist successors of the eighteenth and nineteenth centuries this led to an extreme denial of the existence of innate ability, and an unbounded faith in the powers of education. '*C'est donc uniquement dans le moral qu'on doit chercher la véritable cause de l'inéqualité des esprits*' (15), maintained Helvetius, who held that all men are born intellectually equal. This view became common among progressive educators and school teachers. Jacotot went so far as to state that 'the smallest child has the same intellect as the adult Archimedes' (16). The famous English schoolmaster, Dr T. Arnold of Rugby, believed that it was in energy and moral character that boys differed one from another rather than in intellect. Even Charles Darwin was influenced by these commonly held views until his cousin, F. Galton, began to provide contrary evidence.

Throughout the nineteenth century faculty psychology was under a cloud, though in the first half it still had its adherents in the Scottish and French schools. Herbart in 1816 called the tune when he stated that the soul had 'no capacity nor faculty whatever, either to receive or to produce anything' (17). The dominant viewpoint was well expressed by Taine, whose book *On Intelligence* (1869) appeared just as psychology was beginning to become an experimental science. Psychology involved an analysis of complex mental states into their sensory components, and a discovery of the laws of their combination. Ultimately simple events alone are real. Thus 'the words faculty, capacity, power, which have played so great a part in psychology, are only convenient names by means of which we put together, in distinct compartments, all facts of a distinct kind: these names indicate a character common to all the facts under a distinct heading; they do not indicate a mysterious and profound essence, remaining constant and hidden under the flow of transient facts. This is why I have treated of cognitions only, and, if I have mentioned faculties, it has been to show, that in themselves, and as distinct entities, they do not exist' (18). So 'just as the living body is a polypus of mutually dependent cells, so the active mind is a polypus of mutually dependent sensations and images, and in the one case as in the other, unity is nothing more than a harmony and an effect' (19). In other words, no soul, no capacities, no potentialities. Even psychologists, who like J. Ward and G. F. Stout in Great Britain, had rejected many of the basic tenets of associationism and sensationism, still showed no inclination to return to faculty psychology. 'Such words as potentiality, faculty, susceptibility, are mere marks for our ignorance' (20) held Stout. While J. Ward, the leading British theorist of the late nineteenth century, proposed a 'single subjective activity' to replace 'the objectionable faculty psychology' (21). With this rejection went a disinterest in individual differences. 'Psychology as science', stated J. Sully, 'has to do with general facts and truths of mind. It takes no account of individual peculiarities' (22). It was in this vein too that Wundt regarded J. M. Cattell's concern with individual differences a scientific irrelevance. There was little theoretical basis in the established nineteenth century psychology either for the concept or for the measurement of ability.

Two forces led psychology to the study of the real human individual as he functioned and behaved in society; firstly the establishment in western Europe and North America of highly organised industrial communities, and secondly the development of the biological sciences.

The influence of the new forms of society in creating a demand for a more realistic and practically applicable psychology is commonly underemphasised in the histories of psychology. The essential consideration was that in the new societies the care of the individual ceased to be merely local and personal. The new societies began to count and to classify; they were forced to provide universal education, and were forced to make provision for a growing number of casualties and misfits. Great Britain was the first country to industrialise, though not always the first to introduce the social reforms which industrialism demanded. The first comprehensive census of the population was carried out in 1801. A select committee of the House of Commons in 1806 made a first attempt to collect statistics of insanity. The Lunacy Act of 1845 was the culmination of a great period of reform in the care of the mentally deranged, and the Public Health Act of 1848 established new standards of public hygiene, accepting the principle that the health and well-being of the population was a matter of public concern. In 1870 elementary education was finally made compulsory, a matter in which Great Britain had lagged considerably behind other countries. It was in the context of this new social concern for the welfare and development of individual members of the community, manifested throughout the western world, that the authorities towards the end of the century began to turn for help to the new breed of psychologists. It was the approach of the city of Breslau which led Ebbinghaus to construct his completion test for intelligence in 1897, and of the French Minister of Public Instruction that led Binet and Simon to compile their famous scale of 1905. In Great Britain the pioneering work of Cyril Burt was done on behalf of the education authority of the London County Council. The development of differential psychology, therefore, was on one side a response to the new demands of society.

On the other side differential psychology was the outcome of developments in the biological sciences and in medicine. Eighteenth century naturalists like Linnaeus and Buffon had introduced a new precision into the description and classification of living forms, and dared to include man as part of the *systema naturae*. There was room for a precise, naturalistic description of human types, more exact and scientific than the literary descriptions of the characterologists (La Bruyère, Thomas Overbury, etc.).

This was the inspiration behind Gall's (1758-1828) system of phrenology, an important landmark in the rise of differential psychology. 'Man must be studied as a being of creation: and his nature requires the same method of examination as every natural object—observation and induction' (23). Thus Gall's disciple, Spurzheim. The job of studying human nature was one, not for the metaphysician, but above all for the medical man, who was acquainted with all types of human being in health and disease, and who could relate observations of character and behaviour to anatomical structures. Gall was an indefatigable and often acute observer, and one of his primary interests was in human individuality. His psychology was crude, but, as G. Allport pointed out, it struck a new note. All previous faculty psychologists, following Aristotle, had aimed to establish universal faculties, but 'Gall sought with the aid of his faculties to account for the differences between men' (24). Gall's list of faculties may have been unsystematic, arbitrary and unconvincing, and his mind-body correlations absurd, nevertheless he helped to change the terms of reference for psychologists by opening up new fields of enquiry. A nineteenth century British appreciation is perhaps of some interest.

'A century or half a century ago, it seems to have been a prevailing notion that men are not naturally adapted by mental constitution to one pursuit more than to another; but that when any such peculiar aptitude is evinced, it is due to the direction given to the mind by casual events or surrounding circumstances. In unison with this view, it was expressly maintained by Dr Samuel Johnson, in a well-known passage, that true genius is a mind of large general powers accidentally determined in a particular direction. Phrenology, while failing in its more ambitious attempts, has greatly assisted in dissipating such erroneous views of human nature and by the instances which, partly in the mistaken estimates of its own proper scope, it has industriously brought together, of extraordinary aptitude for music, mechanical invention, calculation, language learning, and other pursuits, as well as peculiar proneness to certain emotions and sentiments, it has widely spread the conviction that there is an infinite variety in the degree and combination of constitutional qualities by which men are adapted to a great variety of functions and fortunes' (25).

Simultaneously with the spread of phrenology, developments in psychiatry, in which the French school emanating from Pinel (1745-1826) and Esquirol (1772-1840) was prominent, led to a number of conclusions which had a bearing on the concept of aptitude. Firstly, Esquirol differentiated intellectual defect, or idiocy, from insanity (26), and described degrees of feeblemindedness varying along a continuum from normality to low-grade subnormality. Secondly, it became clear that although defectives were to some extent trainable, it was too optimistic to hope that they could be brought up to full normal levels of functioning. The wild boy of Aveyron, discovered in 1798, never became normal in spite of Itard's efforts, and in spite of current theories which held that all defect resulted from environmental deprivation and could be removed by educational treatment. Even Seguin (1812-1880), who did much both in France and later in America for the training of mental defectives, had to moderate his early optimism. Methods of training, like Seguin's well-known form-board, could also be, and later were, used as methods of assessment. At least in certain types of defective there seemed to be inherent limits to development, inherent limits of capacity. Thirdly, mental diseases of certain kinds could diminish capacity, and it was suggested this diminished capacity could be hereditarily transmitted. Propagated by Moreau de Tours (1804-1884) (27) and B. A. Morel (1809-1873) (28) these views had considerable currency in the nineteenth century, including the idea of the *dégénéré supérieur*, the pathological nature of genius (29) which culminated in the theories of Lombroso.

In short, early nineteenth century clinical psychiatry confronted psychology with a range of intellectual functioning, which appeared to depend on inherent capacities, but which could be diminished by adverse environmental, organic and hereditary factors. Gradually, toward the end of the century psychologists began to get interested in these phenomena. That they were prepared to do so was the result largely of evolutionary theories and the work of Francis Galton (1822-1911).

Evolutionary psychology was launched four years prior to the publication of Darwin's *Origin of Species* (1859) by Herbert Spencer's *Principles of Psychology* (1855), in which Spencer maintained that 'mind can be understood only by showing how mind is evolved': Mind, for evolutionary psychology, was biological in its foundations. Mind had evolved to the human level through a series of stages, the higher and more complex resting on the lower and simpler. The function of mind was one of adjustment, the 'continuous adjustment of internal to external' upon which survival depended. Functions did not depend upon structures, but, on the contrary, structures derived from and were the product of functions. Aptitudes and capacities, therefore, including intelligence, were functionally formed organisations which had become structuralised because they were advantageous, and were hereditarily transmitted. It was Darwin who provided the factual evidence in support of evolutionary theory, and who pointed to the significance of intraspecific variations in the process of evolution.

Though Darwin himself made a number of significant contributions to psychology, it was his cousin, Francis Galton (1822-1911) who developed the implications of evolutionary theory in the field of differential psychology. Galton's achievement was first to provide evidence for the hereditary nature of human capacities; secondly to apply the idea of statistical distribution, which he derived from Quetelet, to mental faculties; and thirdly to devise techniques, later termed by J. M. Cattell 'mental tests', for the measurement of individual differences in capacity. Galton's genius in establishing the foundation of differential psychology has been almost universally recognised. He saw the problems and he devised the rudiments of the statistical and experimental techniques for supplying answers. The comparative poverty of the psychological basis of his work has not always been so clearly recognised. Galton measured, but he had no very clear idea of what he was measuring. In his earliest article on a psychological topic (30) he simply stated 'talent and character are exhaustive; they include the whole of man's spiritual nature so far as we are able to understand it'. His ideas were in fact confused and vague. 'By natural ability I mean those qualities of intellect and disposition, which urge and qualify a man to perform acts that lead to reputation. I do not mean capacity without zeal, nor zeal without capacity, nor even a combination of both of them without an adequate power of doing a great deal of very laborious work' (31). Galton never amplified this outline statement. He provided no theory of talent, no theory of character. And when he came to measure, he based his techniques on the orthodox sensationalist psychology of his day, which strictly interpreted made no room for the concept of talent at all.

The deficiencies of Galton have not yet been made good, at least in the field of 'talent'. The problems of differential psychology were first systematically set out by Binet and Henri in their famous article '*La psychologie individuelle*' (1895) (32). They discerned two major problems: how psychic processes vary from individual to individual, and how different psychic processes were related to each other in a single individual. Binet and Henri suggested that not all psychic faculties were equally important, and that the mental tester must endeavour to measure directly the 'superior psychic faculties', which in effect meant the more complex, rather than the simple sensory functions to which the early testers had directed their attention. But what were these 'superior psychic faculties'? Binet and Henri set out a list of ten such faculties, but how exactly these were derived they do not explain. Later Binet in his '*L'étude expérimentale de l'intelligence*' (1903) endeavoured to provide observational and experimental evidence of a qualitative kind as to the essential nature of intellectual processes. Yet when he came to construct his scale Spearman, not without justice, described his procedure as 'hotch-potch' and without consistent theoretical foundations.

Spearman's own attempt to make good the deficiencies of his predecessors is well-known, and constitutes a milestone in the study of ability. Spearman's strength sprang from his realisation that both concepts and methods, both theory and techniques, were essential in any scientific enquiry. In factor analysis he provided psychology with a new technique, which has become one of the stocks-in-trade of the psychologist. He conceived 'factors' as a replacement for 'faculties', which he saw more clearly than most psychologists as the necessary foundation of differential psychology. Without faculties there would be chaos (33). The trouble with faculties was the subjective way they had been arrived at, and for this factor analysis provided an objective, scientific substitute. In his subsequent theorising Spearman was less successful, but at least he saw the need for theory to buttress technique (34). Something needed to be said about the factors that emerged from the statistical mill, and an attempt made to fuse together the work of the experimental and applied psychologist and the general body of psychological theory. The theories he proposed, however, 'mental energy and engines' and 'noegenesis', proved much less acceptable than his factorial technique. The former have been quietly dropped; the latter has provided the seeds of many subsequent developments.

Meanwhile differential psychologists have pushed ahead, usually without much concern for theory. Order, hierarchical or multidimensional, has been derived *post hoc*. 'The structure of the intellect' has been made to look tidy. The whole procedure has been justified in terms of 'constructs'. 'A factor is a construct, not a mental element' (35). The system works: it shows 'what goes with what' (36). It enables predictions of a sort to be made. In a recent book entitled *Human Intelligence* (37) theory was briefly dismissed by saying that abilities are traits, and intelligence 'the broadest and most pervasive cognitive trait'. No consideration was given to the unsatisfactory theoretical basis of the doctrine of traits.

The fact is, of course, that, as Ryle (38) pointed out some years ago, both 'ability' and 'trait' are dispositional terms, and dispositional terms are merely 'inference tickets'. To say that glass is 'brittle' means that '*if* it is, or ever had been, struck or strained', *then* 'it would fly, or have flown, into fragments'. To say that a man is intelligent, similarly means *if* he is confronted with a problem, *then* he tends to react in an intelligent way. Correlations are simply quantitative measures of these dispositional tendencies.

So far so good; but looked at scientifically a 'disposition' is nothing more than a low-level empirical generalisation. Its explanatory value may be, most likely is, negligible. The most obvious empirical generalisations are usually scientifically valueless, and the advance of science often depends on the discarding of surface characterisations. Thus physicists made no progress until the 'four elements', into which things could most obviously be classified (earth, air, fire and water), and the four corresponding properties (or traits?)—dry, cold, hot, moist—were thrown into the rubbish-bin. The 'brittleness' of glass can only be explained, not in terms of correlations or the observation of concordances, but in terms of molecular and atomic structure. The establishment of 'dispositions' must give way to the establishment of 'explanations', if science is to progress.

Gradually psychologists are becoming aware of this requirement. 'It is not a sufficient condition', wrote Miles (39) 'for asserting the real existence of a factor that correlation coefficients between tests should form this or that pattern.' And this, he suggests, means identification in terms of genes, neurones, or what not. Perhaps Burt has been an exception in that he has always attempted to link his factorial work with a Sherringtonian model of the nervous system, but his theoretical suggestions have never been very fully developed (40). More recently, as Wiseman has pointed out (41) there has been some *rapprochement* between learning theory and the psychology of abilities and aptitudes, a *rapprochement* of which Ferguson's 1954 article was an early indication.

In spite of these *rapprochements* the gap has not been filled. We still remain without an adequate theoretical basis for the concepts of aptitude and capacity. Psychologists have relied on their intuitions, and on the relics of Aristotelian and faculty concepts embedded in common language and popular thinking. They have either dismissed the need for theory, or been content with something so lightly drawn that it can hardly be taken seriously. Until this gap has been filled, until the concepts of aptitude and capacity have been integrated with general psychological theory, mental testing will remain an empirically based technology, which lacks full scientific respectability.

A. D. B. *Clarke and Ann M. Clarke*

Consistency and variability in the growth of human characteristics*

The topics implied by the title of this chapter are immensely complex, and space will only permit a few of the facts and certain consistencies in the data to be presented. It may be helpful at the outset to outline the argument.

The notion that development, and more particularly intellectual development, was likely to be a linear function of time was in effect advanced in 1913 with the invention of the IQ, although this implication was strongly disputed by Binet. As such the idea of constancy was pure guesswork because no long-term studies could by then have been undertaken. By 1917, however, Sir Cyril Burt noted that, in a group of subnormal children, over a two-year period, IQ constancy was but imperfectly realised, but the early findings of the Terman study suggested a considerable consistency in the development of very bright children. Work in the 1930s by the Iowa Group indicated that growth rates could be considerably affected by appropriate environmental change but these pre-war studies were methodologically weak and many regarded them with considerable doubt following McNemar's attack in 1940. A year later, however, Dearborn and Rothney (1941) published the results of the Harvard Growth Study, a careful longitudinal investigation of physical and intellectual development. These authors concluded that '. . . prediction of growth at various ages is hazardous . . . variability rather than consistency of growth is the rule . . .' On the other hand, much more recently Bloom (1964) has argued that basic mechanisms and processes are likely to be stable and cites non-reversibility, and negatively accelerated growth curves as criteria, with minimal correlations of 0·50 over time for repeat measurements (*op. cit.* pages 3-5). In particular he expects intelligence, academic achievement, generalised qualities of interest and deep seated personality characteristics to be stable.

It is the purpose of this chapter, firstly, to re-examine these apparently very different view-points, and to evaluate data in the areas of intelligence,

* Based on a paper originally delivered to the Education Section of the British Association for the Advancement of Science, September 1970 and further developed in the Sarah Stolz lecture, Guy's Hospital, March 1972.

personality and academic attainment. It will be indicated that there is on the average much more *individual* variability in the growth of these characteristics than is generally recognised, and that a misinterpretation of the implications of correlation coefficients has been largely responsible for the opposing view. It will be further indicated that this variability results both from gradually unfolding genetic programmes and from both gross and subtle environmental influences. Secondly, the implications for reducing the effects of early social deprivation will be discussed in the light of recent work.

Consistency and variability

Genetically, the potentials of the individual and various maturational programmes are completely determined at conception. Their interaction with the uterine environment, however, begins immediately. Maternal infections, toxins or irradiation can have a profound effect upon subsequent level of functioning; so, too, can birth injury, malnutrition or any severe insult to the developing brain (Scrimshaw and Gordon 1968; Clarke 1969). But the genes for a potential IQ of 150 are of little use unless developed; the genetic interaction with gross physical agencies is paralleled throughout later development by interaction with social and psychological factors. The statement that 'intelligence is largely determined by genetics' is as meaningless as a corresponding statement about environment. For each individual there is an absolutely necessary inheritance interacting with an absolutely necessary environment. The more sensible question is the extent to which *differences* between individuals are attributable to a predominance of genetic or environmental factors, and the answer may well be different for different groups living in different circumstances. If we are comparing individuals in virtually identical environments, then environment will not be *seen* to be a relevant variable simply because its influence is equal for all. But such influence could be equally powerful even though differences between individuals under these circumstances may relate entirely to the genetic side of the equation. If, on the other hand, we are comparing individuals from vastly different environments, such backgrounds will be *seen* to be related to their differing status and may be superimposed upon or mask genetic differences between them. The question of consistency and variability in the growth of human characteristics is obviously bound up with these problems and their correlates must be studied if any worthwhile inference is to be made about their causes. Either may reflect environmental

B

consistency or variability interacting with consistent or variable genetic programmes.

In considering the three areas mentioned (intelligence, personality and academic attainments) we shall be discussing the consistency or variability of individual status at two or more points in time, usually reported as group data represented by correlation coefficients. In practice, as R. A. Fisher once remarked, all data are to some extent erroneous and errors of measurement can best be assessed by a repeat measurement shortly after the first has been made. In psychological or educational measurement the immediate retest value we would seek would be represented by a correlation coefficient of 0·9 or thereabouts. The difference between this and perfect agreement between the two adjacent measures indicates the error factor, due in most cases to short-term personal fluctuations of motivation or attention, fatigue, misunderstanding and so on. Anything lower than 0·9, particularly if the coefficient becomes progressively lower the longer the time interval between measures, is unlikely to be primarily due to measurement error but may reflect a real change of status of individuals within the group.

Those unfamiliar with the problems will often blame the measuring instrument for inconsistency over time, so that if a final result were very different from an earlier assessment, one or other would be regarded as being in error. Now of course there are measurement errors in all forms of assessment and it is important to know of their existence and their extent. The same critic of psychological measurement is, however, quite content to report authoritatively on the basis of school examinations that 'John was near the bottom of his class last year and this year is near the top', that is, to recognise that a child's relative scholastic position can alter over time.

There are, as has been indicated, differences of opinion about the extent of consistency and of variability in the growth of human characteristics. These differences relate not only to the essential growth curve of the particular characteristic studied but to the definition of consistency (consider, for example, the modest criteria of stability adopted by Bloom, *op. cit.*). Much of this depends upon the interpretation of the significance of correlation coefficients.

High correlations give the uninitiated a false sense of security concerning the consistency of measurements. Shapiro (1951) demonstrated this fallacy as follows: 'Let us assume that we have a test with a test-retest correlation of 0·9 and a standard deviation of 16. These data mean that, out of every three children obtaining an average score of 100, one would obtain a retest score of 100, one would obtain a retest score above 107 or below 93 . . . out of every 10 children obtaining an average score on the first test, one child would obtain a score above 112 or below 88 on the second test.'

In order to illustrate this theoretical calculation, some actual data on IQ changes in the mildly subnormal and dull normal adolescents drawn in the main from exceedingly bad or moderately bad early environments may be considered. It had been shown that the worse the background, the better the ultimate progress, often including substantial IQ increases between ages fifteen and thirty. Actual IQ results on 25 such people gave a test-retest correlation of 0·897 for a group which had shown an average increase of 9·7 IQ points over 2¼ years. This high correlation, 0·897, conceals one person who made a 25 point increase, three who increased 16 points, three 15 points, one 13 points, and two 12 points, with fifteen improving by 11 points or less. So 0·897 relates to a group of whom 40 per cent made 12 point increments or more (Clarke, Clarke and Reiman 1958).

Test-retest data have been constructed for 75 people in the same population who show our usual immediate test-retest correlation of 0·948 and to these have been added our real 25; the correlation for the total, the 100, reduces to 0·922, a still very high value. So very high retest correlations conceal minorities who show large changes. These results thus completely confirm Shapiro's theoretical calculations, and indicate the danger of assuming that a high correlation over time necessarily implies consistency of growth by all members of a group. As will be seen when the research findings are examined, correlation coefficients much lower than 0·9 are often quoted as showing consistency in development. Thus Bloom (1964) as noted, regards a correlation of 0·50 or above over a considerable period of development as indicating the existence of a stable characteristic. This value implies that each measure accounts for only a quarter of the other's variance. Kagan and Moss (1962) appear to subscribe to the same view. Anderson (1963), however, is even interested in correlations averaging 0·1. Correlations of 0·5 imply a considerable change of status of many members of a group, and we would describe this as being as much variable as consistent. Even a correlation of 0·7 over only five years of childhood development implies that half a sample will change more (and half less) than 7 points in IQ with 17 per cent rising or falling 15 or more points, and nearly 1 per cent by 30 points either way (Vernon 1955).

Another type of misinterpretation of correlation coefficients is also common. Bloom (*op. cit.*), who uses the concept of 'half-development' of characteristics, perhaps borrowed from the 'half-life' in atomic physics, has been led to interpret his correlational evidence as strongly supporting the importance of the first few years. If, therefore, a correlation of 0·7 between IQ at age four and adult IQ is demonstrated, half the variance of adult intelligence can be accounted for at the former age. 'This fact', writes Jensen (1969) 'has led to the amazing and widespread, but unwarranted and fallacious, conclusion that persons develop 50 per cent of their mature intelligence by age 4!' Bloom's central thesis rests upon such an 'unwarranted and fallacious' argument.

Disagreement about consistency may also arise in relation to the sensitivity or insensitivity of the measuring device. If we divide intelligence into, say, three categories: dull, average, superior, then much greater consistency from period to period will be apparent than if we use IQ points or even standard deviations as our units of measurement.

Research data

Consistency of growth is defined as the maintenance of the individual's status during development in a constant position with respect to his peers. The first major conclusion, which can be kept in mind as the data are examined, may now be stated. It will be argued that the longer the time interval between various measures, the less consistent *on the average* will be the individual's growth, granted an apparently constant environment. Major environmental change may, in addition, promote greater variability over time. As a corollary, we should, on the average, expect any group matched on a particular measure at age Y to be less homogeneous with respect to that measure at a later age Z and indeed if we could trace it back, less homogeneous at the earlier age X.

A second major conclusion is that the earlier a particular characteristic is assessed, the less likely will be its long-term predictive usefulness. This should not be surprising since in early childhood certain qualities of intellect, personality and motivation have not yet emerged and cannot therefore be assessed. Just to take one example, a child who is in what Piaget terms the period of concrete operations may not be assessable in terms of his later ability to deal with formal operations. These two conclusions were reached many years ago with respect to intelligence; it will be indicated that they possess some generality.

INTELLIGENCE

The most outstanding feature of all measures of intellectual ability in its broadest sense is that they show some degree of positive co-variation.

A child who is good at one activity has a greater than chance likelihood of being good at other activities. The general intelligence test attempts to span as wide a range as possible of different sorts of intellectual activity by a complex process of sampling and standardisation.

The first major conclusion was that the longer the time interval between measures of the same individuals, the greater the likelihood of change, that is the less consistent the individual's growth, and figure 1 shows the general findings in this field, illustrating the correlation of

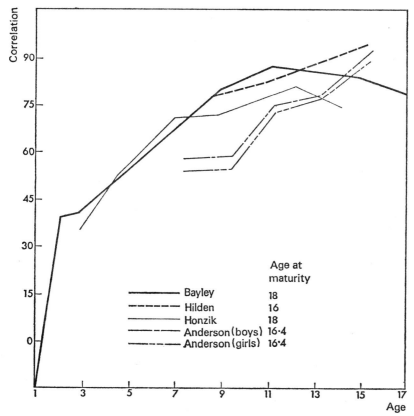

FIGURE I   *Correlations between intelligence at each age and intelligence at maturity; data from five studies. (Bloom 1964. Reproduced by permission of author and publishers.)*

earlier with later IQ measures on five different groups of children. The relationships are barely existent in the pre-school years. They grow rapidly, however, as age increases. Long-term prediction of adult status is impossible from early pre-school tests, and the longer the time interval the less accurate the prediction. Ability to predict future status increases with age, however, as table I also indicates.

TABLE I   *Retest correlations at 3-year intervals*

	Ebert and Simmons (1945) r	Honzik *et al.* (1948) r
Age 2 by 5	—	0·32±0·06 PE
Age 3 by 6	0·56±0·04 PE	0·57±0·03
Age 4 by 7	0·55±0·04	0·59±0·03
Age 5 by 8	0·70±0·03	0·70±0·02
Age 7 by 10	0·76±0·02	0·78±0·02
Age 9 by 12 or 13	—	0·85±0·01

Note increasing correlation with increasing age, test-retest time interval being held constant. Table reproduced from *Carmichael's Manual of Child Psychology* by kind permission of John Wiley & Sons, Ltd.

It will be observed, with test–retest time interval held constant at three years, the coefficients increase with age. In other words, intellectual growth gets more consistent and less variable. Careful studies by Sontag, Baker and Nelson (1958) have, however, underlined the highly idio-syncratic nature of individual growth curves. 'Some individuals had periods of loss in IQ followed by a gain, other cases had periods of gain in IQ followed by a period of relatively little change, and others had still differing patterns of change' (*op. cit.*, page 53).

So far, data from studies of children living in their own homes and under rather constant environmental conditions have been considered; one notes here Bloom's (1964) contention that much of the stability he reports is really a reflection of environmental stability. We will reserve for later discussion what happens when children experience major environmental change. We will also postpone any attempt at considering why growth tends to be variable over long periods of time.

PERSONALITY

In general, personality measurement is more difficult and less reliable than intellectual measurement, and there are fewer long-term studies of the same individuals.

It is clear from published work that some aspects of early personality measurement do not show long term continuity, while others do. One study by Macfarlane, Allen and Honzik (1954) quantified behavioural assessment gained by parental interviews concerning the child's behaviour at 21 months, at yearly intervals up to 16 years. Between age 4 and 16 years, the average inter-correlation for introversion-extraversion was 0·5 for boys and 0·34 for girls. Kagan and Moss (1962) have reported a thirty-year study from birth to maturity, using a variety of personality measures. They state that their most dramatic finding 'was that many of the behaviours during the period 6 to 10 years, and a few during the period 3 to 6, were moderately good predictors of theoretically related behaviours during early adulthood' (see figure 2).

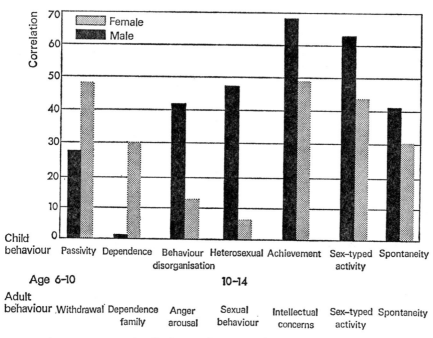

FIGURE 2   *Summary of relations between selected aspects of child behaviour at age 6 to 10 years and phenotypically similar adult behaviour. (After Kagan and Moss 1962. Reproduced by permission of authors and publishers.)*

Note the sex differences in the degree of association between these child-hood and adult measures and that the coefficients range from zero to 0·68, on the average being close to the relationships reported by Macfarlane *et al. (op. cit.).*

Now most of these correlations are significant statistically and cer-tainly indicate some consistency of personality attributes in the early years of schooling with similar attributes in adulthood. But they also indicate considerable change. It is interesting that these findings also have a bearing upon the role of early childhood for later development. If it were true that the pre-school years were as formative as is commonly supposed, then a study of children's personalities in the relatively constant environmental conditions of their own homes might be expected to indicate great consistency of personality attributes during later development. This is not so; few measures before age six showed long-term consistency. In a Minnesota study, Anderson takes comfort in the fact that since child to adult correlations average about 0·1, 'some relation exists between measures made in early childhood and measures made in adult life'. Only 44 per cent of his correlations were above 0·1 and only 13 out of 1672 were 0·5 and above. Similarly, Livson and Peskin (1967) describe the relations between personality ratings at four periods of development (5-7; 8-10; 11-13; and 14-16) and data from adult interviews and assessments of mental health. Only the early adolescent measures proved to be effective predictors of adult psychological states.

Thus, in the field of personality measurement the findings resemble at their best those on intellectual development—little relation between pre-school and adult measures but a growing relationship during childhood, indicating some degree of consistency and some degree of variability in the growth of personality attributes. Quite often, however, long-term personality predictions are very poor indeed. Motivation, being an aspect of personality closely related to achievement, will be considered separately.

This is an important though somewhat nebulous concept and one which is most difficult satisfactorily to measure. Perhaps the best known approach is that originated by McClelland on the need for achievement as inferred from the fantasy productions of children in response to story telling requirements in certain test situations. Feld (1967), for example, retested a group of boys aged 14-16, some six years after an initial measure. In a gross way there was some consistency; those who at age 8-10 had scores above or below the median tended to be similarly placed six years later. That this degree of consistency even though significant was small, however, is indicated by the correlation of 0·38 between the two sets of scores.

Moss and Kagan (1961) report a rather different approach. They rated achievement behaviour at ages 0-3, 3-6 and 6-10. These ratings reflected 'the degree to which the child tended to persist with challenging tasks, games and problems. . . .' Adult ratings were provided by the junior author who had no knowledge of the scores of these individuals when children. These adult ratings described the individual's concern with task mastery in his job as well as in other pursuits, with his attempts to obtain status and social recognition and with the value he placed on intelligence, knowledge, academic achievement and intellectual superiority, regardless of whether the goal was to satisfy inner standards or to obtain social recognition.

For the males, no significant correlation with adult achievement behaviour occurred before the period 6-10; for girls significant correlations appear in the period 3-6. In both, these correlations were around 0·45. Another study by Kagan and Moss (1959) on the stability of achievement fantasy over time shows a decreasing relationship between scores at age 8 with those at 11 and 14. Once again a growing but not very impressive consistency as age increases may be noted.

ACADEMIC ATTAINMENTS

Next, the consistency and variability in the growth of academic attainments must be considered. Here there is a vast correlational literature and merely a few examples will be outlined. Figure 3 indicates the general relationship of achievements over time.

Hockey (1968) reports on the school careers at Marlborough College of over 500 boys between ages 13 and 18. French results at age 13 only correlate 0·49 with O level French marks; Latin yields a 0·53 correlation over the same period; English 0·33; history 0·33; geography 0·32. The only 13+ scores that show correlations of above 0·28 with the number of O level passes were mathematics (0·49) and IQ (0·45). Correlations between age 13 scores and A level passes were even lower, ranging with one exception between 0·11 and 0·24. The IQ score was the exception, yielding a correlation of 0·47.

Unimpressive though significant correlations between A level and University Degree results are also commonly reported and even at postgraduate level, by which time one might have imagined that considerable consistency would have developed, there is a far from perfect relationship between degree class or college performance and subsequent achievement. Wiseman and Start (1965), for example, followed up teachers five years after completion of their training. There was a lack of agreement between college assessment and the headmaster's assessment of the teacher five years later. The authors conclude that 'it may be that the colleges and headmasters are using different criteria in assessing teaching ability and teachers in general. One might expect such criteria differences. . . . Similarly, the professional experience of each teacher must have varied considerably during the five years since he qualified and thus modified his behaviour. Hence differences . . . were to be expected, but it is the magnitude of such differences that is surprising.'

It is clear that the growth of academic attainments over time is subject to quite considerable variability in many cases. It is usually characterised in individuals by cycles, fluctuations or long term trends, up or down.

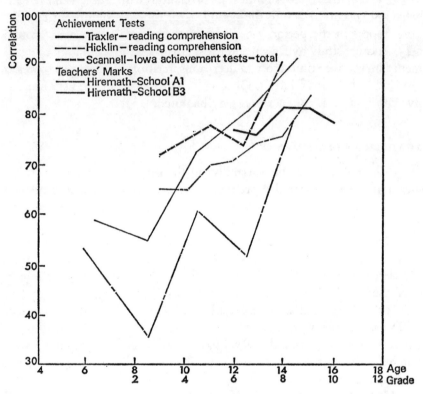

FIGURE 3   *Correlations between achievement at each age with achievement at age 18; data from five studies. (Bloom 1964. Reproduced by permission of author and publishers.)*

THE OUTCOME FOR ORIGINALLY HOMOGENEOUS GROUPS

The reader may recall the suggestion that a homogeneous group should become less so as the time interval gets longer, because individuals within a group will exhibit some degree of variation in subsequent growth (see figure 4).

Here are some individual cases of children who happened to be identically tall or identically bright at a particular age (Dearborn and Rothney 1941). It will be noted that subsequently their scores diverge, and that in the case of the physical measures these are also less homogeneous earlier.

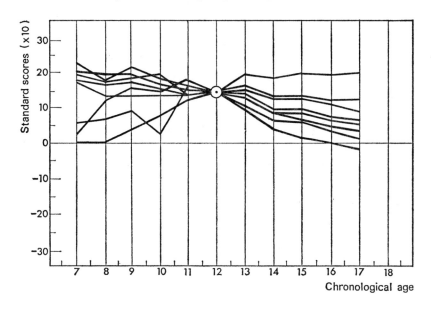

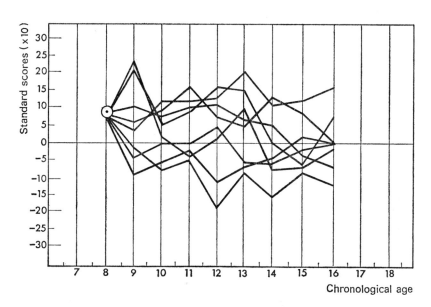

FIGURE 4   *Changes in relative stature of eight girls who were 1·5 sigma above the mean stature of 266 girl subjects of the Harvard Growth Study at age 12 (top graph). Variability in mental growth in terms of standard scores of eight girls who were 0·9 sigma above the mean of 256 girl subjects of the Harvard Growth Study at age 8 (bottom graph). (Reproduced from Dearborn and Rothney 1941.)*

At the lower end of the intelligence range, Baller, Charles and Miller (1967) have reported on the status in middle-age of a large group judged mentally deficient in the late 1920s. These had all attended 'opportunity rooms', had IQs below 70 and were drawn from poor circumstances. Outcome has been immensely varied, with the group as a whole doing much better than had been predicted, and the majority functioning as dull-normal. An extreme minority was institutionalised, and at the other extreme, one man managed his own business.

Similarly, Charles and James (1964) have reported on the present status of a small group of average children who had IQs between 96 and 103 at age 6. On follow-up twenty-seven years later the IQ range now extended from 90 to 132, a dramatic illustration of the facts to which we have drawn attention.

Oden (1968) has given the most recent report on the Terman group, selected from IQs above 140 and high attainments in the early 1920s. Although this group has, as a whole, done outstandingly well, not all members fulfilled their brilliant promise and from adolescence onwards there was increasingly divergence between the most and least successful children. Some details will be offered later in this chapter.

These three studies therefore confirm the general point about growth variability where sensitive measures are used. However, the data also indicate that, on the whole, children brought up in their own homes tend to remain within a general wide band of ability and accomplishment, and thus actuarial predictions can, with exceptions, be made. Similar divergences occur in follow-up studies of psychiatrically deviant groups, although to varying extents depending on the nature of the original deviant condition (Robins 1966; Thomas, Chess and Birch 1969).

Reasons for Consistency or Variability

So far, then, a certain amount of consistency and a certain amount of change during development has been demonstrated. This statement of averages conceals an array of individual differences. Some individuals show a rock-like consistency, maintaining a constant IQ, or a constant position in their classes, constant motivation and so on. Others show dramatic fluctuations, improvements or deterioration with respect to their peers. Most lie between such extremes (see also Sontag, Baker and Nelson 1958).

Most of the findings so far mentioned relate to children brought up by their own parents in relatively unchanging environments. This might suggest therefore, that variability in normal development is mediated by genetic programmes or by rather subtle environmental influences or more probably by both. It seems likely, for example, that in the normal nutritionally adequate and constant environment, a child's physical growth changes are entirely programmed genetically but equally clearly depend also upon adequate nutrition. In such an environment, growth *differences* between children must necessarily reflect genetic differences.

Hence, having shown some degree of variability and some degree of consistency in the development of the characteristics which have been discussed, and the emphasis on one or the other will depend both upon the particular characteristic and the strictness of one's criterion, the final part of this paper will attempt an assessment on the modifiability of development by environmental agencies. Studies relating primarily to the IQ will be considered since these are by far the most numerous, probably because the IQ has been assumed to have a very much closer relation with achievement than appears to be the case. As Vernon (1970) indicates 'intelligence scores are achievement measures just as much as are reading or arithmetic scores. . . . The former does not "cause" the latter. At the same time (they) are useful predictors in so far as they sample the more general conceptual and reasoning skills which a child has built up largely outside school and which he should therefore be able to apply in the acquisition of more specialised skills in school.'

By now, almost all authorities, including Jensen (1969) in his famous article, accept that change from extremely adverse environments into better ones tends to be followed by desirable changes in behavioural characteristics. Jensen's article was written with the aim of explaining the failure of most programmes of compensatory education for the culturally disadvantaged. In it, he singled out genetic factors as primarily responsible. Our own conclusions are somewhat different.

Since, then, there can be no doubt that the effects of gross adversity can to some quite marked extent be reversed, little further attention will be paid to these studies, and more subtle environmental changes and their possible effects will be considered. Before so doing, however, we must indicate a main weakness in Jensen's argument. 'There can be little doubt', he writes, 'that moving children from an extremely deprived environment to good average environmental circumstances can boost the IQ some 20-30 points and in certain extreme rare cases as much as 60 to 70 points. On the other hand, children reared in rather average circumstances do not show an appreciable IQ gain as a result of being placed in a more culturally enriched environment. While there are reports of groups of children going from below average up to average IQs as a result of environmental enrichment, I have found no report of a group of children being given permanently superior IQs by means of environmental manipulations. This suggests that the influence of the quality of the environment on intellectual development is not a linear function. Below a certain threshold of environmental adequacy, deprivation can have a markedly depressing effect on intelligence. But above this threshold, environmental variations cause relatively small differences in intelligence. . . .'

We suspect that Jensen has 'found no report' simply because there are few existing studies of children in average environments being moved to superior environments (see, however, Husen 1951). It seems, therefore, that the so-called threshold effect may be an artefact due to a lack of such research. Note, too, that most of the evidence on recovery from environmental deprivation is derived from studies of children who were *totally removed* from adverse circumstances.

It is certainly true that most of the Head Start intervention programmes in the United States have failed to produce permanent gains in the culturally disadvantaged, and indeed these results were predicted on general grounds in 1967 before many of them were announced (Clarke 1968). But most of these programmes have been pathetically inadequate, amounting to a few hours every weekday for a period prior to entry into a ghetto school in a poor area. They have been, with some notable exceptions, too diffuse, and above all they have not been subsequently reinforced. As Jensen admits, there are exceptions where Head Start programmes are intensive and sharply focused (Bereiter and Engelmann 1966; Gray and Klaus 1970; Heber and Garber 1971). These exceptions are now sufficiently well documented and consistent to indicate both why the majority of programmes have failed and also the necessary ingredients for success. Furthermore, it is by no means universally accepted that training for intellectual gain is more appropriate or effective than concentrating on the achievement of academic and social skills.

Having, as he believes, disposed of environment except for extreme deprivation, Jensen has no need to discuss the many studies on more subtle social influences. Is there any good evidence that such social and interpersonal factors affect development? This is an extremely difficult question to answer firmly. The fact that intelligent, academically achieving children tend to be born to families offering a rich and stimulating environment, and that stupid, poorly achieving children tend to come from culturally and materially impoverished families can be, and indeed is, often interpreted as due either to the overwhelming effects of genetic factors or to the overwhelming effects of environmental factors. No crucial answer to our question can arise from these data.

The clearest evidence that subtle interpersonal factors do affect important aspects of development emerges from the many studies showing that first-born and only children have a significant advantage over later born children in terms of achievement, a phenomenon first recognised by Galton in 1874. Schachter (1963) has reviewed earlier studies of relationships between birth order and eminence and birth order and intelligence, concluding that eminent people are far more likely to have been eldest or only children than to have been later born. No clear answer concerning the relationship with intelligence emerged. Bradley (1968), reviewing later evidence on first-born of both sexes in universities and colleges throughout the United States, showed that these and only children are consistently and massively over-represented. Detailed studies of the finalists in National Merit Scholarship competitions showed among the top half per cent of the population in successive large groups there was a 23 per cent over-representation of first-born and only children. The fact that first-born and only children are over-represented in American universities could be established because of the widespread policy of requiring birth order data for university admission. Comparable data for Britain are not available because ordinal birth position is not recorded on UCCA forms. Unpublished studies in the Psychology Departments of Sheffield and Hull Universities, however, confirm these findings. Altus (1966) after considerable research into the pre-eminence of first-born and only children in academic attainment reported that he was unable to find a single study that showed a divergent trend. More recent writers have added to the picture (Chittenden, Foan and Zweil 1968).

Douglas (1964) has indicated that first-born children stay at school longer, join more clubs, read better books and push themselves harder than other children. The first born of two or three children, particularly from working class families, won far more grammar school places than would be expected from their ability scores alone. Douglas, Ross and Simpson (1968) show that the virtually all-round superiority of elder than younger boys in the same family is established and maintained from about age 8 onwards. Douglas did not, however, find that only children were as a group superior. This leads him to a somewhat different interpretation than is offered in the American reviews, although both have in common the assumption that personality variables relating to need for achievement are involved (see also Sontag, Baker and Nelson 1958). Since the numerous American studies show that the phenomenon includes only children, this interpretation emphasises adult-child relations while Douglas stresses sibling relationships. So far attempts to link this phenomenon with biological factors such as maternal age have not been impressive. It seems much more likely, therefore, that it is due to subtle social influences which differentially affect children growing up in the same family.

Much other work points in the same direction and suggests that slow but consistent environmental forces play a considerable role in determining the rate and type of development, although many such studies yield evidence which allows vastly different interpretations. The classic

TABLE 2   *The Terman A and C groups*

	Education			Occupational Status	
	A	C		A	C
Ph.D. or other doctorate	34	1	Group I		
M.D.	9	0	Professional	59	5
LL.B.	13	6			
M.A./M.Sc.	15	1	Group II		
Other graduate qualification	1	0	Official, managerial, semi-		
College graduate study			professional	40	13
without degree	4	9	Group III		
Bachelor's degree	16	23	Retail business, clerical,		
1-4 years at college			skilled trades, etc.	0	62
without degree	5	26			
High school plus			Group IV		
professional or technical			Agricultural and related		
courses	1	14	occupations	1	0
High school graduation	2	16			
Less than 4 years high			Group V		
school	0	4	Semiskilled occupations	0	8
			Not employed or less than		
			full-time employment	0	12

Data relating to the 100 most successful (A group) and 100 least successful (C group) males in the Terman study. (After Oden 1968.)

Terman study of gifted children selected in 1921 for IQ 140 and above also yields important findings. Oden (1968) has reported an heroic forty-year follow-up of this group. It may be recalled that, as with the follow-up of average and subnormal children, this gifted group has ultimately presented a picture of greater heterogeneity on all measures. Because of this Oden made a detailed study of the 100 must successful (the A group) and the 100 least successful (the C group) men. Let us consider a few of the findings, remembering that all subjects originally lay in the top 1 per cent of the population, and that all ratings and tests were made years before their ultimate allocation to the two groups (see table 2).

Early scholastic records show little difference between the groups, although a difference in intelligence scores was apparent within this highly gifted group. However, As were more accelerated than Cs, finishing both

8th grade and high school at reliably younger ages. The groups began to diverge in high school with the As excelling not only in school marks but also in extent of participation of extra-curricular activities. The most powerful correlates of vocational success were: a home background in which parents place a high value on education, encourage independence and initiative, and expect a high level of accomplishment. So far as subject characteristics were concerned, the As showed better mental health and all-round social and emotional adjustment, and, in particular, perseverance, self-confidence, ambition and integration in working towards goals.

The author concludes that intellect and attainment are far from perfectly correlated and that emotional stability and a composite of the personality traits that generate a drive to achieve are also necessary for outstanding achievement among intellectually gifted men. Thus Binet's hope of making potential scholastic ability predictable by intelligence tests alone has been but imperfectly realised.

There is space for just one further example. In a recent book, Pidgeon (1970) considers the whole fascinating question of expectation and pupil performance. Among the interesting studies he reports is one which shows that 'the vigour, purpose and tempo of the work can also exert an influence that is strongly reflected in the achievements of its pupils.' Having taken a battery of intelligence and attainment tests in primary schools, a random sample of pupils having birthdays in a particular month of the year remained in these schools for a further year while the remainder moved on to secondary schools. A year later both groups were retested; the results showed consistently that children remaining in the primary schools made gains in every test, while those who moved on made losses. Gains and losses were greatest for the brighter children and least for the below average. The effects were most marked in Arithmetic and least so in English, with intelligence coming in between. Pidgeon interprets these results as showing that the schools—and here he means the teachers—had different interests in the purpose of the testing, which was to determine the children's suitability for education in selective grammar schools. 'While this was a major focus in the primary schools,' he writes, 'it was only incidental in the secondary schools.'

Conclusions

An attempt must now be made to draw the many threads together and summarise:

1.   The development of the three groups of characteristics we have considered all tend to show rather similar degrees of consistency and variability over time. As a corollary, groups selected for homogeneity on a particular measure will tend to become more heterogeneous with respect to that measure (and indeed other measures) as time passes.

2.   If the measures of change are crude, then consistency will appear to predominate; if sensitive instruments are used then variability will be the more striking.

3.   In either event, the earlier the first measure and the longer the period over which measurement takes place, the greater the likelihood of individual variability.

4.   This statement of averages conceals wide variations in individual growth rates. A minority maintain a rock-like consistency over long periods with respect to their peers, another minority show marked changes.

5.   Correlational studies are predominant in this field and yield much valuable information. Yet, on their own, their results are often misinterpreted. A correlation even of 0·90 describes a situation in which a minority may make considerable changes in growth rates. A correlation of 0·50 which is fairly typical for measures over, say, an 8-10 year period of development, is one where variance in one of the measures only accounts for a quarter of the variance in the other. While this implies a far better than chance consistency it would seem to us to indicate greater variability. In any event, experimental studies are needed to elucidate correlational findings.

6.   There is no doubt that gross changes of environment are on the average reflected in considerable personal changes. Studies of this sort have been reviewed elsewhere (Clarke 1968; 1970) and indicate that such variability can take place throughout development and is not limited to the early years. To say that the first few years are crucial determinants of the future ignores evidence on the later reversibility of the effects of social deprivation, and overlooks the fact that genetic programmes underlying many cognitive and personality characteristics have not at this stage unfolded. These latter presumably need certain conditions in the social environment to facilitate their full growth. Why, then, the usual emphasis on the disproportionate influence on adulthood of the early years, an extreme environmentalist view? As Vernon (1964) puts it '. . . a likely reason for the emphasis on early experience in depth—psychological theories is that patients like to talk about such experiences as a defence against facing their current difficulties . . .' One might add that clinician and patient probably serve as mutual reinforcers in discovering early anomalies in development; theory may have been imposed on fact.

7.   There is also very suggestive evidence in the study of first-born and only children that subtle environmental influences can promote powerful effects within the same family. Such findings go some way to casting light upon otherwise ambiguous findings relating to social class or home influences.

8.   In growth of all kinds, the interaction of powerful genetic forces and powerful environmental forces are at work cumulatively over long periods of development. In optimum environments, genetic factors will appear predominant and environment will appear less important because its influence is roughly constant. In sub-optimum environments, environmental effects will appear more obvious.

9.   The notion that the characteristics of the disadvantaged can be transformed by a few months exposure to middle class nursery school procedures is pathetically misguided. Long duration, intensive and total intervention, including changes in family attitudes and circumstances are necessary if such children are to be fully assisted.

10.   The environmental factors leading to under-achievement or indeed 'over-achievement' will repay closer scrutiny and study. A genetically potential IQ of 150 is of little value to society if largely unused. Real equality of educational opportunity is a will-o'-the-wisp while inequality remains in the homes. And by inequality in the home we do not especially imply an inequality in material factors but also, and perhaps more powerfully, an inequality in attitudes to the child, attitudes to education and attitudes to life which in combination appear to exert continuous and long term influences upon psychological growth. These inequalities do not merely reflect the differing practices of different social classes but also occur within classes, and indeed also appear to occur within families.

11.   The developmental sciences offer evidence in, as yet, rather broad terms, which enables the environmental circumstances favouring or disfavouring the full development of human genetic potential to be, in an actuarial sense, prescribed. One of society's problems is to learn how to use this knowledge, particularly since evidence points to the crucial importance of long-term domestic environments over which, unlike schools, society exercises little control.

Finally, to summarise the summary, the facts appear to demand modification of many dearly held clichés which, for example, stress that the child is father to the man in the sense that early experience dictates a pre-determined course of development and makes or mars the child. Even education, which from primary school to university is adept at planning the self-fulfilling prophecy, cannot arrange for human development to be necessarily consistent, and if our expectancies do not blind us to the facts, the passage of time provides many surprises, good and bad, about particular individuals. These changes involve the interaction of both genetic and environmental factors. Our growing knowledge of the latter provides some hope that ultimately we may reduce significantly the waste of human potential which is so characteristic of the world in which we live. In the present period the beginnings of methodologically and psychologically adequate work are being witnessed.

Acknowledgements   This chapter was prepared during the author's tenure of a generous research grant from the Association for the Aid of Crippled Children, New York. Dr Godfrey Harrison assisted with statistical and computing problems.

*Stephen Wiseman**

Environmental handicap and the teacher

The majority of teachers are favourably disposed towards educational research, and understandably so since it seems logical to believe that its main result will be to make the task of the teacher easier and more effective. They tend to see as the function of research the provision of the best teaching method, the best curriculum, the best organisation and structure, supported by objective and rigorous proof. The writer has argued elsewhere that this is too simplistic and naïve a view: it immediately raises the question of 'best' for what? Educational objectives are many and varied. Some methods will show themselves best for some objectives (e.g. cognitive learning); others for rather different aims (e.g. personality development). The interpretation of 'best' will depend upon our order of priorities, our pattern of emphases: research does not and cannot absolve us from final value judgments for which we ourselves must remain responsible.

This commonly held view of the role of research as the servant of a kind of educational consumers' association, recommending the 'best buy', is grossly limited in quite another dimension. The concern of research in comparative studies of methods, curricula and structures forms but a small part of its total commitment, and an essentially superficial part at that. The answer to the question 'which?' if it does not at the same time give at least a partial answer to the question 'why?' labels the activity not as research but development. Research—by any reasonable definition— seeks the why and the how by searching for an understanding of the underlying mechanisms mediating human learning and human development.

Although educational research has an apparently long history, stretching back to the early years of this century, its progress has been slow and difficult. Only since the last war has anything but a derisory level of financial support been given to it, even in America—and in Britain government money (apart from a trickle through the side-door of university departments) was not provided until the last decade. All this means

* Professor Wiseman died before he was able to correct the proofs of this chapter.

that educational research is in its infancy, that insights are few and scattered, that a coherent body of theory is as yet barely in view, and that for some considerable time to come it will be constrained to operate a probing and exploratory role. In such a situation it is courting disappointment and frustration to pitch one's expectations too high. The results of research projects, even the most comprehensive and expensive, are likely to be the disclosure of unexpected complexities and apparent inconsistencies, rather than the provision of irrefutable truths. The importance of this should not be under-estimated. The results of such explorations are to be found in the posing of new questions to answer, and the re-phrasing of old questions in new forms. The effect of these on educational opinion and educational policy can be quite profound: even in its exploratory phase research can, and should, have significant influence on planning and policy.

For the teacher, however, far from research making his task easier, it seems to increase his difficulties. This it does by uncovering complexities, hitherto unrecognised, lying beneath apparently simple situations. The researcher throws new light on existing problems, demonstrating that traditional approaches are at their best only partial, since they ignore hitherto unsuspected factors; and yet, since knowledge of the underlying mechanisms is lacking, he is unable to offer firm advice to the teacher on how to restructure his methods and techniques.

Educational retardation

In no area is this dilemma more obvious than that of educational retardation, particularly when it is associated with social and cultural deprivation, whether this refers to pupils from the depressed areas of our cities, or to immigrant pupils from developing countries.

When the writer began his teaching career over forty years ago, in charge of a backward class in a North London elementary school, the problem of backwardness appeared a relatively simple one. Diagnosis and treatment were seen as (almost) entirely cognitive matters. It was the beginning of the age of testing. The development of standardised tests of attainment made it possible for the teacher to have much more accurate knowledge about the level of attainment of his pupils, expressed in terms of reading age, mechanical arithmetic age, spelling age, etc., by reference to norms secured from large and representative samples of pupils. Thus the degree of backwardness of any child could be assessed with considerable accuracy. But the teacher had an even more powerful weapon in his armoury alongside these attainment tests—the group test of intelligence. Here, he was assured, was a measure of innate capacity, revealing a mental age which, when set alongside the attainment age and the chronological age, permitted a diagnosis and indicated a treatment. It was all deceptively simple. Chronological age 10 years, mental age 10 years, reading age 8 years; diagnosis, 'merely backward'; treatment, remedial teaching. Chronological age 10 years, mental age 8 years, reading age 8 years; diagnosis, 'dullness'; treatment, nil (since he is 'working up to capacity'). One even had the analysis: chronological age 10 years, mental age 8 years, reading age 10 years; treatment, 'take off the pressure, he is achieving too well'!

The situation sketched above is certainly over-simplified, and yet it remains a true picture of the views of the vast majority of teachers during the 1930s. Educational psychologists are often bitterly attacked for their part in producing what is now seen as an educationally counter-productive treatment of the slow learner, but this, for many of them, is less than just. Sir Cyril Burt—the focus of most of the attacks—produced four major books in this period: *Mental and Scholastic Tests* in 1921, *The Young Delinquent* in 1925, *The Subnormal Mind* in 1935, and *The Backward Child* in 1937. In all of these (and, naturally enough, particularly in the last one) stress is laid on the multi-causality of backwardness, and the importance of personality factors and environmental effects as well as cognitive efficiency. The average teacher, however, does not form his opinions and base his methods on the study of such solid fare: they are formed by his training college tutors, and developed and re-structured by lectures and short courses run by LEAs and teachers' associations, as well as by the 'how to do it' articles in the teachers' journals. With few exceptions these pre-war sources of guidance adopted the simplified cognitive approach and the mental age/attainment age basis of diagnosis and treatment. The effect of this, as we now recognise, was disastrous. A significant proportion of the school population was condemned to languish, without help and without hope, at the 'bottom of the class', apathetically—or resentfully—serving out their wasted time until they attained blessed release at fourteen.

Not all teachers were tarred with the same brush, of course. Those in charge of special classes for backward children, in contrast to their colleagues responsible only for a handful at the tail-end of a more heterogeneous 'normal' class, could hardly fail to suspect the simplicity of this approach in the light of the wide variety of response and reaction from their putatively homogeneous pupils. The present writer was fortunate. As a graduate, trained to teach physics in a grammar school, he found himself thrown in at the deep end, facing twenty-five backward Cockney sparrows from a severely deprived neighbourhood. He sought help from London University's evening classes, and sat at the feet of Spearman, Burt, Aveling, Flugel and Percy Nunn. These mentors—and even more Lucy Fildes, of the Canonbury Child Guidance Clinic, to which he had referred one or two of his problem cases—provided a perspective and a stimulus which was very necessary. The problems of communication and under-standing faced by one brought up in a northern mining village, and pitch-forked into a southern urban community of similar socio-economic level but a very different culture pattern led him to the study of anthropologists like Malinowski and Margaret Mead, and laid the foundations of what was to be a permanent interest in environmental and cultural factors and their effect on education.

No apology is made for spending time and space on what might seem to some an unnecessary historical prelude to the meat of the chapter. It is important to recognise the stages in the development of our under-standing and our educational methods. There are still many teachers in our schools who continue to accept this limited analysis of backwardness and its causes, and still more who find it difficult to escape entirely from its pervasive effects. It is doubtful whether our in-service training pro-grammes adequately recognise this fact, or that local authorities are suffi-ciently aware of the profound effects one or two such teachers may have in certain schools. And where it is the head of a school who embraces such a jejune philosophy, the consequences are all the more pervasive.

The widening perspective

The move away from this preoccupation with cognitive factors began in earnest during the last war, and can be seen as part of the national urge to plan a better, juster and more civilised society once the holocaust was over. The influence of the massive evacuation programme for school children, which opened the eyes of countless inhabitants of villages and country towns to the realities of life in the slums of our great conurbations, cannot be overestimated as a significant element in building up this determination for social change. This dramatic face-to-face demonstration of the acute environmental handicaps afflicting thousands of the nation's children added impetus to the egalitarian mood of the country and to the call for equal opportunity for all. The armed forces themselves provided clear evidence of the failure of the education service to recognise and nourish ability and potential. In contrast to the First World War, personnel selection was developed in the Services from the outset, and the results from the tests used for allocation demonstrated that among those who had left elementary school at the earliest possible moment was a surprisingly high proportion of talent and ability which had remained unrecognised in the schools. Routine follow-up studies in the Services confirmed the validity of such test results, and there must have been (and still are) many thousands of men holding post-war jobs of responsibility and influence who, had it not been for the war, would have languished in much lowlier and less demanding occupations.

All this focused attention on *educational opportunity* and the inequalities in this. Tribute must be paid to the sociologists (rather than the psychologists who, by and large and with some obvious exceptions, remained surprisingly impercipient and inactive in this area) for a number of influential researches carried out during the 1950s which had profound effect on educational thought and policy.* The studies of Halsey and Gardner (1953), Spinley (1953), Glass (1954), Floud, Halsey and Martin (1957), among others, demonstrated very clearly that the tripartite system set up by the 1944 Education Act had failed to achieve the equality of opportunity hoped for by its originators, affected as they were by the emphasis on cognitive, testable factors. Parallel with these sociological investigations came a large number of researches on the selection process for grammar schools. These revealed what the psychologists saw as a very high level of efficiency (expressed as a correlation coefficient) but which the critics, looking at the percentages of children misclassified, regarded as an unacceptably inaccurate process of identifying—irreversibly—second class citizens. At the same time there were increasing numbers of research papers by psychologists which made it clear that intelligence tests, like tests of attainment, were influenced by environmental factors, and that it was no longer justifiable to regard the IQ as a measure of innate ability. To Hebb's differentiation between Intelligence A (innate potential, the capacity for development) and Intelligence B (the average level of performance by the partly grown or mature person, under the influence of environmental opportunity) was added Vernon's Intelligence C (the fallible measure of B). Such developments were powerful attacks not only on the philosophy of the tripartite selective system of secondary education, but also on the previously accepted dichotomy between 'backwardness' and 'dullness'.

---

* This emphasis on post-war developments should not be allowed to obscure the fact that some individuals were concerned with environmental factors and inequalities of opportunity during the pre-war period, but their influence was slight. See the writer's *Education and Environment* for a review of the literature up to 1963.

Environment and attainment

All this research, as well as others such as the Ministry of Education's *Early Leaving* Report (1954), was concentrated on educational *opportunity*, which was attacking organisation and structure, and thus led to the move towards comprehensive education. The study of the effect of environment on educational *attainment* was slower in its development. This was partly because of the time necessary for the educational psychologists to adjust their priorities (or, as their critics might say, rearrange their prejudices), but mainly because of the greater difficulties in this field. The obsession of English education, since the war, with structure and organisation, was a direct result of the emphasis on educational opportunity. This is the field of operation of the administrator and the politician, with the teachers sitting uneasily—and largely helplessly—on the sidelines. Since the majority of the population rejected selection at eleven years and gave general approval to the concept of comprehensive education, conflict between the major political parties on education was never fundamental, but was confined to local skirmishes on such matters as rate of progress and the relative virtues of different patterns of 'comprehensiveness'. Because of this emphasis on structure, however, many politicians, sociologists and even educationists came to believe that reorganisation, of itself, could produce immediate and significant changes for the better, even though the same pupils (although rearranged and regrouped) were being taught in the same buildings by the same teachers using the same materials. A number of researches in the 1960s, however, re-emphasised the crucial role of the teacher, and demonstrated how, by his underlying philosophy, shown in his expectation of pupil performance, he could nullify the intentions of the reorganisers.*

It is only by research into the effects of environment on educational attainment that we are likely to produce results directly relevant to the task of the teacher in the classroom, and to suggest methods which are likely to offset the handicaps of deprivation and disadvantage. Early studies in America and in Britain (e.g. Chauncey 1929; Shaw 1943; Burt 1943) showed a significant correlation between educational attainment and socio-economic level, and post-war researchers were equally attracted to this particular relationship. Few other variables have enjoyed such intense popularity. Unfortunately the results of such enquiries yield little in the

* See Burstall (1968) for the effect of teacher-expectation on the learning of French by below-average primary pupils; Barker Lunn (1970) for the effect of 'streaming teachers' in unstreamed classes. A recent book by Pidgeon (1970) describes other studies offering similar evidence.

way of new insights into 'why?' and 'how?', since the differences within social classes are much greater than those between them. Socio-economic level and social status are units too coarse for productive enquiry. Fortunately the 1950s and 1960s produced a series of research studies which grew in sophistication of technique and comprehensiveness of coverage. Multifactorial studies were mounted, and regression analysis and factor analysis employed in an endeavour to tease out the complex inter-relationships among a large number of variables assessing different aspects of home, neighbourhood and school environment. We are still very much in an exploratory phase of such research, but a number of significant findings have emerged which are of direct relevance to the task of the teacher and the school. The major post-war* British researches were those of Fraser (1959), Wiseman (1964), Douglas (1964), the investigations made for the Plowden Report (DES 1967). Out of these, and the many American studies, four major findings have emerged.

Crucial research findings

First, it is clear that the effects of the home and of the neighbourhood far outweigh that of the school. This was exemplified most dramatically, perhaps, by the Plowden researches on primary school children, which found the proportion of variance in educational attainment contributed by home factors to be at least four times that provided by school variables. The Plowden follow-up, four years later (Peaker 1971), shows that, in the secondary school, 61 per cent of the variance now displayed was determined at the primary stage, the secondary school contributing only a further 4 per cent. Such results are profoundly depressing for the teacher, and emphasise the necessity for attack on two fronts, one to reduce the home effect, the other to make the school more effective in counteracting social and cultural deprivation. But such attacks cannot be mounted until we know something of the geometry of environmental vectors. This is now becoming clearer, as we shall see.

Second, the major factors in the home which are associated with educational backwardness are not material or economic: they are (*a*) the attitude of the parents to education and to school, and (*b*) the literacy of the home. This finding led the Plowden Committee to the view that here was a very promising approach: if adverse home factors are largely

---

* The paradigm, of course, was provided by Burt's classic multivariate investigation reported in *The Backward Child* (1937). It is surprising that it took so long for this example to be followed.

attitudinal in nature, then let us attempt to change attitudes, since this appears easier than to change economic and material circumstances. This view appears to ignore some important considerations. First, the re-searches of the psychologists over the years have very clearly demonstrated that attitude-change is difficult to accomplish; that change, when achieved, tends to be small; and that change tends to be temporary.

More importantly, perhaps, the Plowden view rests on an assumption that is by no means certain: that a demonstrated *association* between parental attitude and pupils' educational attainment implies an underlying *causality*, and furthermore—and crucially—that attitude causes attainment rather than vice versa. Many secondary school teachers would argue, with specific examples to prove their point, that pupil attainment alters parental attitude towards school. O-level GCE successes often change parents' aspirations and expectations, leading them to support and encourage sixth form studies and the idea of college education. It is at least likely that causality acts in one direction in some cases and at some stages, and in the opposite direction in others. What the relative propor-tions are, we simply do not know. But it is possible—a tenable hypothesis —that with younger children in the infant and junior schools, attitude more often mediates attainment, but that towards the middle and end of secondary schooling a reversal may occur, particularly with the above average achievers. Or, alternatively, it may well be that the pattern is one in which, throughout school life, the under-achievers are handicapped still further by adverse parental attitudes to learning and to school, while the above-average achievers tend to educate their parents to support their aspirations.

Attitudes to school

While one may doubt the judgement that parental attitude can be changed more easily than compensatory and supportive elements in the school can be strengthened, nevertheless it is important to ensure that the schools and the teachers do all in their power to promote positive attitudes in parents towards education and learning. It is clear that the key institutions here are the infant and junior schools, where the young mother, as a mother, first comes into contact with the educational system. Her memories of her own schooling are likely to be less than happy: the chances are that she herself was a slow learner from a deprived home and neighbourhood, and that her school experiences were those of frustration rather than achieve-ment. Her view of teachers will be coloured by her own experiences of them as a schoolgirl, and as a (probably) rebellious adolescent schoolgirl at that. Add to this the almost built-in antagonism and suspicion felt by the under-privileged for the authoritarian middle class, exemplified by the probation officer, by the health visitor, by the council inspector and above all by the teacher, and it will be clear that the infant school and its staff have a difficult job to establish a friendly and co-operative relationship. Only by adopting a welcoming, outgoing, non-critical approach and—above all—making it abundantly clear that *all* children are valued and cared for, can they hope to achieve this. Fortunately our infant schools, above all others, have a reputation for doing just this, and most (but not all) make an excellent start on the job of producing good educational relations. But many junior schools, perhaps even more secondary schools, do less than they might in carrying on the good work.

The recommendations made in the Plowden Report on participation by parents, on parent/teacher relationships, and on contacts between home and school are therefore to be welcomed. The difficulties facing schools in this direction—and particularly secondary schools, where the need is greatest—should not be under-estimated. The formation of a parent-teacher association (PTA) is probably the first move that comes to mind, but many of these turn out to be almost counter-productive when viewed in terms of their impact on the parents of the under-privileged pupils. The ideal comprehensive school, it is said, is one which contains the whole range of ability and the whole range of social class. But this is the most difficult of all in which to establish a really effective PTA. Many a headmaster is familiar with the situation in which the association is run—very efficiently—by the knowledgeable and committed middle-class parents. These are the ones who value education, who have the administrative and organisational know-how, who have the right contacts outside the school with those who are likely to help with materials or expertise or money. It is very satisfactory to be able to report, at the school speech day, how much money has been raised for the television, the tape-recorders, the orchestral instruments, or the swimming pool, but it may well be that the price to be paid for these educational trimmings (many of which are exploited to the full only by the above-average pupils) is the further alienation of the very parents whose co-operation and allegiance should be the primary target of the whole PTA exercise.

It takes a very determined head, with a clear-sighted philosophy and order of priorities, to be able to cope adequately in such a situation. There seems little doubt that whatever the school may do in the way of organising societies, associations or clubs, what matters in the end is personal contact between parent and teacher. Much more exploratory and development work could profitably be done in this direction in the majority of British schools. Working Paper 27 of the Schools Council, *Cross'd with Adversity* (1970) has some good advice on possible methods and approaches.

The early years

The third major outcome of research in the 1960s is the incontrovertible demonstration that environmental deprivation bears most heavily on the earliest years of childhood, and that, before even the child reaches the infant school he is already handicapped in the vital area of language development. If nothing is done to remedy this, he arrives at school unable to take advantage of the opportunities offered, the deficit becomes cumulative, and he is firmly and permanently lodged in the ranks of the slow learners. Hence the development of nursery school programmes such as Head Start in the United States, and the Plowden recommendations for the recognition of Educational Priority Areas (EPA) and for nursery school provision within them.

But setting up nursery schools is only the first step. The real question is, what do we do within them? The British nursery school tradition, originating in the pioneer work of Rachel McMillan and Susan Isaacs, is a famous one. It stems from the philosophy of Dewey and the psychology of Freud. From Freud came the belief that play in childhood had two functions of importance to the educator: a didactic function and a therapeutic one. Through play, the young child learned to come to grips not only with his physical environment but also with his emotional environment. Jealousy, anger, frustration—and how inevitable these are for the pre-school infant—could be 'played out' and so release his energies for intellectual and social development. From Dewey came an analysis of the learning process, with strong emphasis on the motivational element. The child, for Dewey, was not a receptacle for knowledge, but an active seeker after information and skill. The essence of education was the provision of an environment which would prepare the active learner to develop at the optimum rate. The teacher's role was to provide materials and to pose problems—to place the child in a 'forked-path situation'—and to be at hand to help with new material, or with advice and support, when this proved necessary. Both these strands, Freud and Dewey, led to a strong emphasis on the *activity* of the child, in largely unstructured situations.

How successful will such a programme be in remedying the language deficiencies of the disadvantaged child? The answer seems to be, very little. It is an admirable programme for a middle-class child from a tidy suburb, providing him with the activities and opportunities denied to him at home, but most of which are commonplace to the foot-loose and fancy-free youngster from the slums, with little or no parental supervision. It is no doubt true that with such a regime the deprived child's vocabulary is likely to increase somewhat, particularly in its store of nouns. But how important is this? As one investigator* has pointed out, ignorance of the meaning of sheep, or elephant, is unlikely to prove a lasting educational handicap. Ignorance of the meaning and function of such words as *if, but, or, because, since, when*, is a much more serious matter. And experience shows that appreciation and command of language structure cannot safely be left to chance, under the stimulus of free play and activity methods. What is required is a planned and graded attack, using a language programme specially devised to meet the known deficiencies of the disadvantaged child.

To be effective, the EPA nursery school programme must be supported by adequate orientation and training courses for the teachers concerned, otherwise the initiative, the energy and the financial outlay will be largely wasted and the major objective unachieved. Surely, it will be said, we can rely upon the teachers to adapt their methods to this new and challenging task? But can we? A survey of the opinions of a number of nursery school teachers to the structured language programmes which are being used for disadvantaged children has recently been made.† Let me quote some of the comments collected from the teachers. First for balance, a couple of protagonists: 'I think it's tragic—absolutely tragic—that all the children in the nursery can't do it. They all need it so much.' And: 'I know I *ought* to do language every day, but I've never been as systematic as this before. I'm definitely being kept on my toes.' But now listen to these: 'There's quite a few things that are useful, but I'd really rather work in my own way.' And: 'There's a lot of very interesting equipment but we'd rather use it in our way than the directed way.' And: 'I don't like it. I think it's soul-destroying and an insult to my integrity.' And: 'I don't know which side I've fallen down on. The children enjoyed it and certainly learnt a lot. There's no doubt they've improved beyond recognition—but I feel the idea is against all nursery principles.' And, finally: 'It's often a grind to get through it. I look at the lesson and know it's going to be boring and so, of course, when it comes to the lesson it *is* boring. The children don't enjoy it and neither do I.'

It is true that much of the criticism derives from the fact that the programme in common use is American in origin, and that, apart from

* Bereiter, C. and Engleman, S. (1966).
† Quigley (1971).

the chauvinistic reaction to an educational import, it is less than satisfactory in content and approach for British schools and British children. But it is also clear that here we have a strong rejection by many teachers of *any* alteration in the traditional approach to nursery education. The strength of feeling and depth of emotional response is often more appropriate to religious controversy than to educational practice. Educational philosophy has become educational dogma. Rachel McMillan and Susan Isaacs, both responsive to new ideas and concepts, both basing their teaching on the newest developments in educational thought, would hardly approve. How can the training courses of these teachers have left them so inflexible, so unadaptable, so unresponsive to new insights? The educational world is changing around them, but they remain encapsulated within the shell of holy writ. The function of our colleges of education is to produce flexible professionals, adaptable to change and responsive to new demands. Some of them have clearly failed, producing instead missionaries preaching the one true doctrine, arrogantly repudiating any deviation from it. And this is all the more remarkable when one considers that a typical day's programme for nursery school children from deprived areas contains no more than thirty or forty minutes of structured language teaching, with the rest of the day devoted to traditional free activity and play.

Bright children at risk

The fourth research outcome of major significance is the demonstration that, contrary to most popular opinion, environmental handicap bears most heavily on the brightest of our children. 'This finding, which has some support from other enquiries,* is of the greatest significance for educationists, for politicians, and for society as a whole. When we think of the problem of material and cultural deprivation, we see it as a problem affecting the "submerged tenth" of the slum-dwellers, the poverty-stricken. We tend to assume that it affects only the tail-end of the ability-range as well as the tail-end of the income-range. Both of these views are wrong, and the second is even more radically wrong than the first. Educational deprivation is *not* mainly the effect of poverty: parental

* Among British enquiries, note Burt (1943) who found 'decidedly higher' correlations with environmental factors for brighter children than for duller, and concluded that 'it is far more urgent to provide brighter children with an education appropriate to the ability of each than to do so for the dull, the backward or the defective'; Fraser (1959) found a highly significant relationship between ability levels and the effect of home background; Maxwell (1953) concluded that 'high intellectual ability is more widely distributed over different social environments than is low intellectual ability'.

attitude and maternal care are more important than the level of material needs. The child from a home with an income of £30 per week may be more at risk than one from a much poorer home. The assumption that educational deprivation breeds educational backwardness is true but misleading. What is more in accord with the facts is the dictum that educational deprivation *prevents* the flowering of latent abilities, and that the higher the potential, the more potent and the more catastrophic are its effects' (Wiseman 1967). This quotation comes from Appendix 9 of the Plowden Report, yet, curiously enough, no mention is made in the Report itself of this important and significant finding, nor are any of the Committee's 197 recommendations relevant to it. Here is striking evidence of the strength of stereotyping!

The challenge offered to the teacher is a particularly severe one, since he, too, is affected by the stereotyped view. Consider the problem posed by the pupil from one of the worst of our urban ghettoes, with an IQ (A) of 120. Intelligence B—because of his background—is 100, and his teachers find him keeping up with the average. They are likely to regard him as one of their successes since, in spite of his background, he is not backward and retarded. The underlying potential remains unrecognised and unstimulated. How many such languish in our schools? No one knows, but undoubtedly we have here a waste of human resources and a stifling of talent that will continue as long as teacher expectations remain hidebound by traditional assumptions.

Immigrant pupils

There is one area of environmental handicap that needs separate and special consideration: that of the immigrant pupil. The typical Pakistani, Indian or Jamaican child, newly arrived in Britain, is affected by similar environmental handicaps to those of his English neighbour, but with a different pattern of intensity, and with additional stresses and demands. But there is much to be said for viewing his problems within the total scene of social and cultural deprivation, rather than treating them as special and isolated.

The recent survey by Townsend (1971) for the National Foundation for Educational Research in England and Wales (NFER) provides the most up-to-date picture of the British scene. Although the total number of immigrant children in the country is but a tiny fraction of the whole school population, their concentration in particular areas provides special problems for some local authorities. There are many schools with high

C

proportions of such pupils—and very many more with none at all. The survey makes it clear that the response of local education authorities (LEAS) to the influx of immigrants over the past decade has been a varied one in terms of innovatory methods of organisation, but has been remarkably similar in terms of aims and objectives. All have concentrated —to the exclusion of almost all else—on the obvious and immediate problem of language training. This is very understandable, since schooling becomes impossible until means of communication are established, but it is to be hoped that authorities and schools will speedily widen the scope of their activities and recognise, in particular, the importance of parental attitude and cultural differences. There seems little realisation, for example, that the latter can be capitalised on (to the benefit of English pupils and for the reduction of racial intolerance) as well as compensated for.

American research

One of the dangers inherent in British reaction to this very new educational problem is that of a too-easy assumption that American experience and American research and development are directly relevant. This is far from self-evident. The Negro problem in the United States has produced a vast literature and a massive number of enquiries, but the black pupil in a Harlem school has a very different life-history from that of a Pakistani in Bradford, a Jamaican in Slough or an Italian in Bedford. One recent American writer has said: 'Any groups which have been geographically or socially isolated from one another for many generations are practically certain to differ in their gene pools, and consequently are likely to show differences in any phenotype characteristics having high heritability. . . . But such an hypothesis is anathema to many social scientists. The idea that the lower average intelligence and scholastic performance of Negroes could involve, not only environmental, but also genetic, factors has indeed been strongly denounced. But it has been neither contradicted nor discredited by evidence. The fact that a reasonable hypothesis has not been rigorously proved does not mean that it should be summarily dismissed. It only means that we need more appropriate research for putting it to the test. I believe that such definitive research is entirely possible but has not yet been done.' This quotation comes from Jensen's now notorious paper in the *Harvard Educational Review* (Jensen 1969). The storm which greeted this underlines the political implications and emotional reactions attendant on work in this area. Notice that Jensen merely propounds a hypothesis, and suggests that further research should be mounted to test it. For this he is condemned as a racist! We are back with the nature/ nurture controversy, about which the present writer commented in 1964, 'Even to pose the question has been dangerous in certain periods of history; to give a particular answer has been to invite imprisonment, torture and death.' Perhaps we have not progressed as far from the Middle Ages as we thought!

The use of intelligence tests with immigrant children poses even more problems than with the native-born disadvantaged. The search for culture-free tests has largely failed, and many psychologists see this approach as a blind alley.* There are those, too, who—impressed by the evidence that intelligence test scores as well as achievement test scores are depressed by adverse background factors—refuse to see them as anything more than rather specialised attainment tests, and would exclude them as part of any programme of educational guidance. This seems to the writer wholly mistaken. The effects of environment on tested IQ are undoubted, but less than the effects on attainment. And the large number of multi-variate researches using both kinds of test, and demonstrating very clear differences in factor-pattern (and, where relevant, predictive power) between them, make clear that such a non-differentiation is a gross over-reaction. Differences between IQ and AQ are always worth knowing, and noting, *provided that* the lack of any difference is not taken as proof of an adequate level of functioning.

Cross-cultural studies

Having suggested that comparisons with American Negroes may be dangerous, and should be viewed with caution, one must not, by extension, rule out the value of other cross-cultural comparisons. Indeed, in the writer's view, this is an area which—as yet—has been far too little explored. Apart from work by a few social psychologists in developing countries (usefully surveyed by Jahoda 1970) there are only two major attacks in this field. Lesser, Fifer and Clark (1965) have produced a pioneer study of first-grade children from four ethnic groups from middle- and lower-class groups in the USA: Chinese, Jewish, Negro and Puerto Rican. They found very distinct differences in the pattern of abilities as revealed by tests of Verbal Ability, Reasoning, Number Facility and Space Conceptualisation. Figure 1 summarises these differences. The important fact here is not

* Recent work at the NFER (Haynes 1971) suggests that individually-administered tests of learning progress are more useful predictors of future educational achievement with immigrant pupils than tests of intelligence.

so much the differences in level among the ethnic groups, but the clear demonstration that the *patterns* of abilities are significantly different. Comparison on a social class basis showed the expected differences within each ethnic group (with 'more of a difference in the mental abilities of the Negro children than in other groups' between middle-class and lower-class) but the same pattern of abilities was revealed. Lesser *et al.* conclude that further work 'must now incorporate the broader educational considerations of curriculum development, teacher training, and school

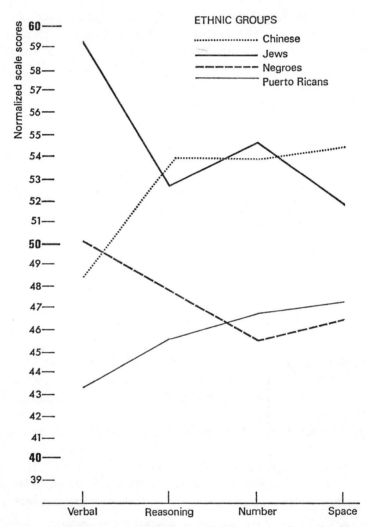

FIGURE I   *Pattern of normalised mental-ability scores for each ethnic group. (From Lesser, Fifer and Clark 1965.)*

organisation. We have shown that several mental abilities are related to each other in ways that are culturally determined. We propose that the identification of relative intellectual strengths and weaknesses of members of different cultural groups must now become a basic and vital prerequisite to making enlightened decisions about education in urban areas' (*loc. cit.*, p. 84).

The only other worker who seems to have taken this suggestion seriously is Philip Vernon himself. For some years now he has been conducting a series of intensive cross-cultural enquiries, involving Indian,

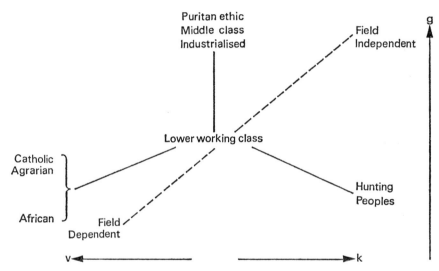

FIGURE 2   *Diagram of dimensions of cultural groups. (From Vernon 1969.)*

Eskimo, Jamaican and Ugandan pupils. The major report published in 1969 is not only an interim report on his own results, but also provides an invaluable overview of research and theory in this area.* His survey of the factors influencing the mental development of children considers genetic influences, nutritional and health conditions, perceptual and language factors, child-rearing practices and parental attitudes, and types of social structure and values. The way in which ethnic groups differ in mental abilities *g*, *v* and *k* Vernon represents graphically (figure 2), which 'shows the western middle class as high in intellectual ability or *g*-factor and "formal" language, and contrasted with the less civilised and with the western working classes. Cutting across this dimension is the spatial-verbal

---

* But, oddly, enough Lesser, Fifer and Clark are not mentioned.

which tends to differentiate hunting from agricultural peo
this does not imply that agriculturalists are necessarily h
ability (unless they also have sufficient *g*), only that they a
better on this than on the spatial side. Witkin's dependence d.
shown as oblique, since it combines elements of *g* and *k*, of mio
ness and of resourcefulness.'

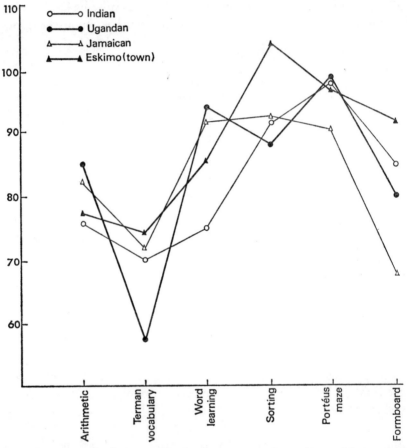

FIGURE 3   *Fiftieth percentile development quotients. (From Vernon 1969,*
table 12, p. 236.)

Vernon administered some twenty-two individual tests to his various
ethnic groups, so that the data he provides are particularly rich—and
complex. Even so, as he himself comments, 'little opportunity was provided for Eskimos to demonstrate their artistic and mechanical abilities,
and none at all for the Ugandans to display their auditory and rhythmic

skills.' His results show the expected differences in the patterning of abilities. To try to parallel the graphs of Lesser *et al.* with so many variables is too confusing, and for detailed results the reader is referred to Vernon (1969, pages 234 ff.). But the present writer has picked out—most arbitrarily—six of the test results to demonstrate visually the kind of differences displayed (figure 3). Interpretation of such differences, and those shown in figure 1, is far from easy; nor can they be fully reconciled with the theoretical structure shown in figure 2. Clearly we are still a long way from more than partial and limited insights. Vernon provides, in his book, a summary of the main factors underlying poor performance on tests, a list which is useful, he suggests, 'in trying to diagnose the underlying handicaps of disadvantaged children, particularly immigrants, in our own culture. They are classified below under three or four main headings to correspond to our distinction between Intelligences A, B and C.

C. *Extrinsic handicaps*

1. Unfamiliarity of testees with any test situation, and lack of motivation.

2. Difficulties due to particular form of items or materials (e.g. pictures), and conditions of testing (e.g. working at speed).

3. Anxiety, excitement, suspicion of tester.

4. Linguistic difficulties in understanding instructions or communicating responses.

B. *Constitutional handicaps*

5. Brain damage due to pre- or post-natal malnutrition, maternal stress, or disease. Birth injury; later brain pathology and deterioration.

Positive environmental factors

6. Reasonable satisfaction of biological and social needs, including exercise and curiosity.

7. Perceptual and kinaesthetic experience; varied stimulation, encouragement of exploration, experiment and play.

8. Linguistic stimulation encouraging a 'formal code' and clarity of concepts.

9. 'Demanding' but 'democratic' family climate, emphasising internal controls, responsibility, and interest in education.

10. Conceptual stimulation by varied environment, books, TV, travel, etc.

11. Absence of magical beliefs; tolerance of non-conformity in home and community.

12. Reinforcement of nos. 8 and 9 by school and peer group.

13. Regular and prolonged schooling, also demanding-democratic; emphasising discovery rather than rote learning only.

14. Appropriate methods to overcome language problems.

15. Positive self-concepts with realistic vocational aspirations.

16. Broad and deep cultural and other leisure interests.

A. *Genetic factors*

17. General plasticity.

18. Genes relevant to special aptitudes.'

The role of the school

How can the schools attempt to overcome these conditions? One of the conclusions from the researches touched on in this chapter is inescapable: that the role of the teacher is crucial. Teaching methods, teaching material, methods of grouping, testing and measurement, all can help and have their due place, but their effects are relatively minor compared with that of the teacher himself—his attitudes, his beliefs about ability and potential, his whole educational and social philosophy. The effect of teacher attitude and teacher expectations on pupil achievement and pupil aspiration is one which operates either for the release or the inhibition of intellectual powers and potential. We are here in the area of *pupil motivation*, where we must recognise that changes in this can have profound effects on achievement and progress. For too long teachers have been encouraged to confine their attention and interests to the level of cognitive ability of slow-learning pupils, seeing this as the major determinant of educational success, and wasting a good deal of time and energy on operationally-futile arguments about heredity and environment. We must come to grips with the certainty that different levels of motivation and stimulation can make nonsense of predictions based on the results of cognitive tests, and that the pupil's energy and drive, his ambitions and aspirations, his response to difficulty and challenge, can be profoundly affected—for good or ill—by the teacher's underlying philosophy and beliefs.

What is required in an educational programme designed to give full opportunity for all, and particularly for the socially disadvantaged and the immigrant? First and foremost, a positive, encouraging and hopeful attitude on the part of the teacher is needed. Let us recognise that the spectrum of political and philosophical beliefs among the teaching profession is as wide as in any other sector of society, that academic Alf Garnetts are not unknown in school staffrooms. For the extremists here, the small minority of reactionary hard-liners, slum children are stupid, lazy and antisocial, immigrants are demonstrably inferior both intellectually and culturally. The school must put up with them, and make sure they are not a nuisance by keeping them occupied with simple, routine tasks. Such teachers form a tiny minority of the profession, no doubt, but the effect of one such in a school endeavouring to cope with sizeable numbers of disadvantaged or immigrant children can be catastrophic. It is unlikely that the attitudes of such extremists can be modified: the essential strategy here is for the local authority to ensure that they are allocated to schools where their attitudes do least harm. This is far from easy, but one has the impression that in many—perhaps most—authorities, such a course of action has never been considered, let alone attempted.

Fortunately the great majority of our teachers are less fixed in their attitudes and opinions, and tend to respond to positive leadership. Here the crucial figure is the head teacher, which emphasises the importance of choosing the right sort of head for inner-city schools. The selection and training of head teachers do not appear to be among the most efficient elements in the educational system, and although there are encouraging signs of a greater concern here, much yet remains to be done. And a relatively small increase in the quality of heads could produce a much larger improvement in education as a whole.

Attitude-change must also be encouraged by in-service training courses. Far too little is done in this direction at present, and what is done is less than adequate in terms of content and type of course, whether this is judged by what teachers say they want, or what research indicates is needed.* In the 1970s, in-service training is almost certainly more important for the efficiency of the education service than is initial training, and yet the funds devoted to it are a tiny fraction of the total training bill.

The second requirement is the use of teaching methods and teaching strategies that capitalise on the particular relative strengths of individual pupils—which implies as full a knowledge as possible by the teacher of what these strengths are. The demonstration of significant ethnic differences in the pattern of abilities underlines this even more strongly. The

* See Townsend (1970) for the results of the comprehensive survey of in-service training, 1967.

teacher must use all the aids open to him, and these must include tests of achievement and of ability—including intelligence tests. *But*—and this is the important point—the results must be used positively, and not interpreted as evidence of 'irremediable dullness'. For the disadvantaged, all test scores are depressed, to an unknown amount, and some more than others. So the teacher cannot rely solely on such measures. He, as a professional, must always be on the alert for the signs and clues of potential and ability, and seek to nourish and stimulate. The patterning effect already stressed calls for as rich and varied an educational fare as can be achieved, not forgetting the areas often regarded as 'trimmings' (particularly in boys' schools) such as music, movement, art and handicraft. Teaching content must be designed to stimulate and feed the interests and abilities of the children: a curriculum of relevance.

Thirdly, what is needed is an authority-structure and ethos within the school that permits and encourages individual development, that offers opportunities for responsibility to all pupils, and that makes it clear to teachers, parents and pupils alike that all individuals are equally valued in their own right. For schools with immigrant pupils this should be extended to the recognition of the worth of all cultures, and a clear differentiation between integration and assimilation. The necessity for stronger home/school relationships and teacher/parent contacts is even move obvious for immigrants than for the native disadvantaged, in order that immigrant parents can begin to appreciate the rationale of educational methods and organisation often so very different from the schooling they themselves knew in their native lands.

The overview of research presented in this chapter—rapid, selective and necessarily superficial—underlines the point made in its opening section that research up to the present has tended to increase the teachers' difficulties rather than resolve them. It uncovers more problems and reveals more complexities, and, as yet, provides little in the way of guidance. This should act as a stronger spur to greater research efforts in this field. Cross-cultural enquiries form one sector of the field that has been unaccountably neglected in comparison with other areas, and yet it is probably the most promising approach for more basic insights. It is fortunate that Professor Philip Vernon is continuing his pioneer work in this direction. Let us hope that other workers will follow his example.

K. *Lovell*

Growth of formal operational thinking

The nature of formal operational thought

Piaget has postulated two levels of logical thought. The first is in evidence around seven to eight years of age in western-type societies and is termed 'concrete operational'. Thought at this level can deal with data that is intuitable, that is, perceptible or imageable, and permits transformations on reality by means of interiorised actions that are grouped into coherent reversible systems. Such thinking permits the child to elaborate, say, the basic concepts of mathematics and science. It must be stressed, of course, that concrete operations function only with reference to observations, or representations of observations, reckoned as true, and not with data which is merely hypothetical. However, around 11 to 12 years of age the child, in Piaget's view, begins to move to the second level of logical thought which is termed 'formal operational'. The essence of such thought is (Inhelder and Piaget 1958) the capacity to invert the direction of reality and possibility so that whereas concrete operations are centred on reality, formal operations deal with transformations which are merely possible.

Having briefly stated the nature of both concrete and formal operational thought, it is necessary to examine the latter more closely. Moreover it will become clearer that in the writer's judgement it is only the ablest children of eleven to twelve years of age that begin to move to formal operations; in ordinary pupils the age is around fourteen to fifteen years.

From seven to eight years of age upwards, the child is increasingly able to carry out first order operations. The operational structures available to him include classifications, seriations, correspondences, also matrices or double entry tables. There are also the infralogical operations which are available to the pupil. These involve space, measurement, time and speed, and they are built roughly at the same time as the logical-mathematical operations. Indeed they are isomorphic to the logical structures, but they deal with continuous objects and are based on proximities and separations, whereas logical structures relate to discrete objects and are based on the similarity and differences or equivalences between the elements. However, the subject eventually meets problems in which he realises that a particular effect may result from several concomitant influences. Experiences are met in which interfering variables give inconsistent or even contradictory results, as when he finds that most large heavy objects sink in water, although some do not while some small light objects do. Clearly new thinking skills are needed to handle this type of problem.

Again at the level of concrete operational thought the child can carry out reversibility by inversion or negation. The inverse operation combined with the corresponding direct action cancels the whole thing: for example, $X - X = 0$. Thus when attempting to isolate the effects of a variable he notes that it is present in some instances but not in others, or he introduces it on some occasions but not on others. For example, in the experiment involving a simple pendulum he will push the latter on some occasions but not on others in order to test for the effects of the push. But the pupil at this stage of thought cannot negate, say, the length of a rod or the weight of an object. Such physical properties cannot be so eliminated, and the limitation of his thinking is immediately apparent. But the adolescent can neutralise a variable of this type for he can carry out reversibility by compensation or reciprocity. For example, if he is comparing the flexibility of rods of varying length and thickness, and of different materials, he can eliminate the effect of length by making the lengths of the rods equal. Furthermore, at the stage of concrete operational thought the pupil is only able to introduce or eliminate a variable in order to see what role it plays. Thus in the pendulum experiment he pushes or does not push the pendulum in order to see if the variable of push is causally effective. But he is unable to consider giving (or withholding) a push each time he changes the length of the wire in order to determine the effect of the variable of, say, length. But in formal operational thought the pupil may eliminate a variable not only to control its own influence, but also when he wishes to analyse the effects of change in a second variable without perturbation due to the first. Thus with the outset of formal operational thought the subject discovers that variables can be separated by both exclusion and neutralisation, and more important, that a variable can be eliminated for the purpose of analysing the changes in other variables.

It was stated earlier that concrete operational thought deals with the direct organisation of perceptual or imageable data. Through the co-ordination of his actions the child structures only the reality on which he acts. It is true that the child can make an extension of the actual in the direction of the possible, but it does not entail his imagining what the actual world would be if some hypothetical conditions were fulfilled. Rather it is a simple potential extension of actions or operations in respect of some specific situation or content. But in formal operational thought the adolescent can produce more complex expectations: he can elaborate a series of hypotheses, deduce the consequences, and after some form of experimentation or further reflection select those hypotheses that are compatible with the evidence. Indeed, the 'facts' are not looked upon as such until the subject has used procedures that pertain to the complete set of hypothetical relations and obtained experimental verifications for the facts. In short, one can say that in formal operational thought the pupil regards the facts in front of him as that sub-set of possible transformations that have actually come to pass. Thus Inhelder and Piaget regard the essence of formal thought as the ability to reverse the direction between reality and possibility. Moreover, as the pupil's thought now moves from what is possible to what is empirically real, formal operational thought is hypothetico-deductive in nature.

After outlining the fundamental characteristic of formal operational thought it is necessary to look at it in other ways. At this stage the pupil no longer deals with objects directly but rather with verbal elements, and so a new kind of thinking—propositional logic—is imposed on the logic of classes and relations relevant to the objects in question. It is, of course, important to note that the function of formal thought is not merely to translate into words and propositions, concrete operations that could have been carried out without formal thought. Rather, as a result of the experimental manipulation of objects or ideas, a whole new range of operational possibilities become available during the early stages of formal thought, these consisting of disjunction, implication, etc. Thus since we are dealing with more than a simple registration of data, Inhelder and Piaget admit that propositional logic certainly needs some inner verbal support. At the same time, however, they deny that the real power of such logic resides within this support; rather it results from the combinatorial power which makes it possible for the pupil to feed reality, as it were, into a set of possible hypotheses which are compatible with the data. This combinatorial power, in turn, is subservient to a still more fundamental characteristic of formal thought, namely the subordination of reality to possibility.

We may also characterise formal operational thought as second degree operations. Indeed, for some purposes in education it is a most helpful way of looking at it. At the level of concrete operational thought the child is able to coordinate his actions upon objects, structure relations between given elements, and so elaborate first order relations. But at the stage of formal operational thought the pupil can structure relations between relations as in the case of, say, metric proportion which involves the recognition of the equivalence of two ratios. Indeed, the position is neatly expressed by Inhelder and Piaget (1958, page 254) when they write 'In this sense proportions presuppose second degree operations, and the same may be said of propositional logic itself, since interpropositional operations are performed on statements whose intra-propositional content consists of class and relational operations'. When we look at formal operations in this way it helps us to understand why concepts such as energy, thermal capacity and mathematical group are not grasped, except intuitively, until the onset of formal operational thought, whereas number, length, temperature (all derived from the coordination of actions on reality) are available to the child in the junior school.

Some further experimental evidence

The seminal book in which the Geneva school outlines its views on the nature and growth of formal operational thought is, of course, *The Growth of Logical Thinking* (Inhelder and Piaget 1958). In this, two broad groups of problems are outlined, the solution to which requires formal thought. One group necessitates that the subject provide proofs of hypotheses through the experimental manipulation of variables; as in the pendulum experiment. The second group demands that pupils discover relationships which involve direct and inverse proportion, and find solutions to tasks which necessitate an understanding of reciprocity in physical systems. It was postulated by Inhelder and Piaget that relationships exist between the thinking skills involved in the two groups of problems through the combinatorial reasoning demanded in both. That is to say, it was argued that the processes in the two groups of tasks operate in terms that can be represented by the same system of relations, namely the four-group (see Lunzer 1968). It is not within the province of the writer to argue with Piaget over the latter's efforts to construct 'logics' corresponding to different levels of thought. However, there is now sufficient empirical evidence available to suggest that these two groups of tasks do indeed share common thinking skills.

Lovell (1961) gave five combinations of experiments, selected from the ten experiments originally used by Inhelder and Piaget, to different groups of subjects aged eight to eighteen years (192 pupils in all). Kendall's

Coefficient of Concordance (*W*) was used as an estimate of the degree of agreement between the levels of thinking attained on the various tasks. The value of *W* ranged from 0·52 to 0·89 depending upon the age range and ability range of the groups of pupils concerned. Jackson (1965) used the experiments of Oscillation of Pendulum, Law of Floating, Conservation of Motion, Communicating Vessels, Falling Bodies on the Inclined Plane and Equilibrium in the Balance, with forty-eight primary and secondary school pupils. Ten subjects responded at the same substage on all six tasks, and just over 70 per cent of the subjects had their replies included within two or fewer substages.

Again the studies of Hughes (1965), and also Lovell and Shields (1967), showed, using principal component analysis, that members from each of the two groups of tasks had substantial correlations with a general intellective factor. More recently Bart (1970) used the tasks of Conservation of Motion, Oscillation of Pendulum, Equilibrium in the Balance and Production of Shadows, a task involving vocabulary, and three paper and pencil tests involving formal reasoning, one each in biology, history and literature. The battery was given to ninety subjects, thirty at each of the ages of thirteen, sixteen and nineteen, all the testees being above average in general ability. Using the Maximum Likelihood method of factor analysis it was shown that the eight measures had a bifactor structure, with a large general factor and a secondary factor that distinguished tasks from tests.

Thus the scattered and varied evidence as a whole gives some grounds for suggesting that the tasks originally proposed by Inhelder and Piaget to demonstrate modes of thinking which they described as formal operational do in fact depend upon common thinking skills. But the size of the correlation coefficients between scores obtained on these tasks depends upon the homogeneity of the group, and on the age of the subjects, for such coefficients tend to increase in size with age. Again, familiarity with the content of a task seems likely to facilitate, markedly at times, the use of formal operational thought in its solution. Credibility, too, affects the elaboration of formal thought in particular situations. For example, logical necessity and initial belief tend to work against one another in the pendulum experiment since such belief due to 'common sense' suggests that the weight of the bob must be a relevant factor. On the other hand, in the experiment involving the sliding bodies on an inclined plane, logical necessity and initial belief augment one another (Lunzer 1965).

There are thus a number of issues which influence the appearance of formal thought when a solution to a task demands it; and such thought is not always equally available across all content areas as in, say, mathematics, history, and political science. Moreover we cannot tell at present whether formal operational thought is just not available in the case of a given task, or whether it is necessary, in addition, to posit some kind of analytic set such as that proposed by Beilin (1969) in respect of the use of concrete operational thought, which in some way activates the subject's cognitive apparatus and allows him to analyse the data inhering in that situation.

The experiments of Inhelder and Piaget used tasks which one meets in the field of the natural sciences. It must not be thought, however, that formal operational thought is found only in that area. Indeed the stages of thought proposed by Piaget are found throughout the curriculum. Hallam (1967), for example, showed that in history, pupils' answers could be classified as pre-operational, concrete operational and formal operational with other replies at intermediate points between these stages. At the level specified as concrete operational the answers show that the pupil can use the information provided but that his thinking is limited to what is immediately apparent in the text; he can move from one point of view to another but cannot coordinate two or more viewpoints; and while he has the capacity at times to forecast the outcome from the evidence provided, he cannot elaborate a mature hypothesis. But at the level of thinking designated as formal operational, the subject attempts to relate the different variables, and realises that a multiplicity of possible links may be at work; he also tries out his thinking in a systematic fashion and goes beyond the given data using hypothetico–deductive thinking.

But it should be said that in respect of history both concrete and formal operational thought are in evidence later than in some other school subjects. This is not unexpected for the pupil encounters actions and situations far removed from his own world, and involving the motives of adults far from him in time and space. Other work carried out under the writer's direction has shown that formal operational thought is in evidence in reasoning about literary and political issues. Goldman (1964) likewise found that the Piagetian stages of thought were reflected in the answers which pupils gave when questioned about Bible stories.

It must not be thought that either adolescents or adults reason at the formal level all the time. Indeed Inhelder (Tanner and Inhelder 1960) makes it plain that 'the attainment of a cognitive stage merely indicates that the individual becomes capable of behaving in a certain way which was impossible before'. Thus the individual is likely to operate at different levels during the day; sometimes at the formal level when he is well informed in respect of the content of the situation, and credibility is favourable; sometimes at the concrete level when the task is unfamiliar; and even at the pre-operational level on occasion. Again it seems certain that a proportion of adolescents and adults do not reach the stage of formal operational thinking, or reach it temporarily in specific and limited situations. What the proportion is cannot be estimated. With changes in schooling and culture more may well reach this stage of thought. It must, however, be a matter for serious concern for democracy (using the term in a western-type sense) that a proportion of adults in an electronic-technological age live mainly at the level of concrete operational thought.

Educators are naturally concerned to know if the growth of formal operational thought can be aided. Unfortunately it is difficult, at present, to be precise on this point. Inhelder and Piaget consider that some minimum level of neurophysiological development is necessary, but over and above this the age of onset of formal thought is affected by schooling, social attitudes and exchanges, and the culture generally. But it is not yet possible to pinpoint the exact features of school and society which aid or retard the move to formal thought. A study in southern Europe led Peluffo (1967) to suggest that lack of schooling and underdeveloped milieu retarded the onset of combinatorial and anticipatory thinking. Again the work of Kimball (1968) in Malawi, involving 36 boys and 36 girls at each grade from one to eight inclusive carefully selected to represent all regions of the country, indicated that the notions of chance and metric proportions is coming late in such pupils. A task for future research will be to establish the exact features in child rearing practices, and in schooling and in society generally which aids the growth of formal operational thought (see the work of Vernon, 1969, in respect of the growth of thinking in younger pupils). Studies going on under the writer's direction at the time of writing do not suggest that different teaching methods in a particular subject area and lasting one school year greatly affect the rate of elaboration of formal thinking in respect of that area of knowledge.

We have seen then that formal operational thought can tackle possible transformations, and it can assimilate reality in terms of deduced and imagined events. This changed outlook influences the affective as well as the cognitive life, for the values of the individual need no longer be related to the untuitable, but may now be linked to social and interpersonal relationships as well. Indeed, not only is the adolescent capable of forming theories about the world and the way in which it should be run, but he may join a particular group or organisation, or choose a career, which will enable him to foster his aims for, say, social reform.

Elaboration of the scheme of proportion

In this section a brief discussion of the elaboration of the scheme of proportion is included since metric proportion is so important in mathematics and science. As already stated, metric proportion illustrates formal operational thought in the guise of second order operations.

With the onset of concrete operational thinking around 7 to 8 years, the child increasingly notices, with age, certain regularities in his environment. For example if $x = f(y)$ and $x^1 = g(y^1)$ where f and g indicate certain regularities ($f = g$ is a special case), there will exist relations between x and y, and between x^1 and y^1. But there will also exist relations of relations such as x is to y and x^1 is to y^1. Thus if we put $x = $ toe, $y = $ foot, $x^1 = $ finger, and $y^1 = $ hand we obtain items which might be found in an analogics example within a verbal reasoning test.

Such relations of relations are not, in Piaget's view, true proportions for there is no equivalence between crossed products. He speaks of these as examples of pre-proportionality and this may explain why examples of this type can be worked by junior school pupils who have no ability to handle metric proportions. However, these pre-proportionalities give way to an operational treatment of relations between relations and eventually to the notion of proportionality in the strict sense.

Piaget *et al.* (1968, chapter 3) have described some interesting experiments regarding the development of the scheme of proportionality. These are as ingenious as we have come to expect from the Geneva School and the findings are at least suggestive, although they are in need of confirmation. In one experiment the child was shown three 'fish', A, B, and C, which were, respectively, 5, 10 and 15 centimetres in length. They were described as eels so that length could be increased without a corresponding increase in girth. A number of 'balls of meat' were available (up to 50) and it was the subject's task to give a suitable number to each fish on the assumption that the strength of the appetite of the fish corresponded to its length. In a second task the child had to give 'biscuits', represented by little rulers which appropriately varied in length, corresponding to the lengths (appetites) of the fish. It should be noted that the unit meat balls were discontinuous, and the little rulers continuous in respect of their unit lengths.

The following questions were asked using appropriate language:

1.   If one ball is placed in front of fish A, how many do we give to B and to C?
2.   If fish B gets four balls, how many are needed for A and for C?
3.   If fish C gets nine balls, how many are needed for A and for B?

The questions were then asked again but in terms of biscuits, so that in the rephrased question 1 the fish was given a biscuit of unit length.

It is said that the children's responses fell into four broad stages. In the first the child makes a judgement of 'more 'or 'less', so that almost any number of meat balls or any length of biscuit will suffice providing fish B has more than fish A, and fish C more than fish B. This 'qualitative proportion' is really only a kind of qualitative correspondence. With the onset of the second stage, numerical quantification begins in an elementary form. The subject perceives only a qualitative or ordinal property between the ranks of the fish A, B, C and the order of the qualities of food A^1, B^1, C^1. At this stage the relations between relations B^1 is to B as A^1 is to A and so forth, seems to be expressible only in the simplest cardinal form of $B^1 = A^1 + 1$, $C^1 = B + 1$. Moreover, this stage comes rather earlier in the case of the balls which are discontinuous unities than in the case of the little rulers.

In the third stage the subject uses pre-proportions which are more complex than those of the ordinal type but which are not yet true proportions. The type of pre-proportion used is what Suppes has termed 'hyperordinal'. In an ordinal scale one places $B > A$, $C > B$ but without knowing how much greater; while in metric proportionality we know the difference between A and B, say, *a*, also between B and C, say, *b*, and we can express the relationship between the differences in the form $b = na$, etc. When using a hyperordinal scale one is, as it were, half way between. One can compare the intervals between A and B as 'more' or 'less' than the difference between B and C. The subject's pre-proportionalities are of the form *a* is to a^1 as *b* is to b^1 but in which the equality of cross products is missing. Finally at the fourth stage true metric proportionality is realised and the relations between relations are understood.

It has long been known that many children by nine or ten years of age can tackle arithmetic progressions which depend upon additive compositions. They can also work many verbal analogies since they are a kind of pre-proportionality. But many studies, such as those of Inhelder and Piaget (1958), Lovell (1961), Lunzer (1965), Lovell and Butterworth (1966), Steffe and Parr (1968), confirm the lateness in pupils' ability to handle metric proportion—around 11 or 12 years of age in pupils of outstanding ability and around 15 years of age in average ones. Some of the studies just listed provide much evidence of pupils' attempting to use 'differencing' before metric proportions.

Very interesting, too, is a study by Shepler (1970). He investigated the possibility of teaching a unit of probability and statistics to twenty-five sixth-grade pupils of average and above average ability, from a middle class area in the mid-West of the USA. Pre- and post-tests were given, but only three of the items used will be discussed here. After the teaching programme there was a 100 per cent response to the problem:

Spin the spinner on the right *two* times. What is the probability of getting a '2' on the first spin and a '4' on the second?

In this pupils are dealing only with simple intuitive data and the problem can be solved by multiplicative classification. It can, therefore, be successfully tackled by pupils with flexible concrete operational thought. But it was possible for only thirteen pupils to give the correct reply to a question involving estimated probability.

Example   In 6000 spins of the spinner at the right, Bob gets 2653 reds. What is the estimated probability of getting a red on the next spin?

Even so some pupils may have obtained the answer in rote fashion knowing that the probability must be < 1. In another question involving an estimate of a probability using large numbers only seven pupils obtained the right answer. These two items were the only ones in which the percentage number of correct replies was unsatisfactory. They were also the items not dealing with intuitive data, and for which formal operational thought was necessary. Such a study clearly brings out what aspects of probability can be taught to pupils and what cannot before the onset of formal thought. In the Shepler study it would seem that some of the sixth-graders must have been moving to formal operational thought.

Conclusion

The teacher will be well repaid if he analyses the ideas which he wants his pupils to understand, and listens carefully to the arguments they adduce. If he takes both together, he will be better enabled to judge whether an idea can be grasped at an intuitive or analytic level. Piaget's notion of formal operational thought has thrown much light on the growth of pupils' understanding in all areas of school work.

H. J. Butcher

Divergent thinking and creativity

Human creativeness, its correlates in other kinds of ability, the circumstances in which it matures and can be fostered, the kinds of temperament to which it is most commonly allied—all these topics were extensively pondered long before psychology as a science was thought of. Positive and negative aspects of creativity were recognised very early. Any society, to avoid stagnation, needs a constant supply of original ideas at all levels; but the profoundly original men, who are the most fertile source of these ideas, are often the very people who most disturb society by threatening its established ways of thought and familiar structure. Plato recognised this and was so conscious of the seditious potentiality of poets and artists that he banished them, though reluctantly, from his ideal state. The threat is still felt in the twentieth century. Einstein, Russell, Sartre, Robert Oppenheimer, Chomsky, Pasternak, Solzhenitsyn—these and many others of equal eminence have at one time or another been *persona non grata* to the established authorities of their respective countries and sometimes to the majority of their fellow-citizens.

The sociology of creativity and the study of how innovations and inventions are received and disseminated is an absorbing and generally neglected topic in spite of interesting contributions by Kuhn (1962) and Rogers (1962). Although the theme of this essay is the study of originality and creativity in the individual, it would have been misleading not to point out that this is a small part of the total picture. The field reviewed will indeed be narrower still, principally to reflect the main focus of psychological research during the last twenty years, which has been concerned with cognitive aspects of creativity and primarily with those that can be quantified.

'Creativity' has been a fashionable topic of research for fifteen to twenty years in the USA and for less than a decade in the United Kingdom. Much of its popularity, as Foss has pointed out, has developed for non-psychological and non-scientific reasons. Nevertheless this wave of interest, though describable to some degree as a fashion, has generally been beneficial. The study of abilities appeared to be stagnating, both because tests were constructed within too narrow a frame of reference and because the cognitive and affective domains were too sharply distinguished (Heim 1970); for these and related reasons few of the brightest young psychologists were being attracted to the whole field. The increased interest in creative ability has had an ameliorative influence in all these directions.

It has perhaps produced more effect in the first of these respects (new kinds of test) than in the second (less rigid cognitive/affective division). There is however a strong *a priori* case, supported by a fair sprinkling of research, that, whether at an everyday level or in terms of exceptional scientific and artistic production, creativeness depends not only on cognitive but also on temperamental and motivational dispositions. The latter kinds of trait are very probably of at least equal importance although harder to assess objectively; for this last reason there is therefore less to report in the shape of replicable research findings. The work of Roe, Barron, Mackinnon, Cattell, among others (see Vernon 1970) is suggestive and, considering the very different techniques used, reasonably congruent, but wells have been sunk only in scattered parts of the oilfield. Even in the USA, the main effort has been devoted to cognitive aspects rather than temperamental, and in this country the latter kind of study has hardly been attempted.

Most 'creativity' research during the last fifteen years has not only concentrated on the cognitive aspects of the topic, but has been strongly influenced by the 'structure-of-intellect' model of J. P. Guilford, in particular by his formulation of a set of abilities under the general heading of 'divergent production'. A consequence has been that many psychologists have equated 'divergent production' abilities with creativeness, and have often gone a great deal further in this direction than Guilford would go. Four assumptions have commonly been made, none very satisfactorily supported by the available evidence: (*a*) that high ability on tests of divergent thinking is evidence of creativeness in real life as shown by, for example, scientific or artistic achievement; (*b*) that the various measures of divergent thinking inter-correlate sufficiently highly to justify the assumption of a general factor of divergent thinking; (*c*) that a general factor of this kind is readily distinguishable from the corresponding factor of convergent thinking; (*d*) that the resulting bivariate distribution is bimodal, so that we can usefully classify people as 'convergers' or 'divergers'.

There is a degree of paradox in the way Guilford's pioneering work in model-building and in the construction of tests has been applied;

whereas he has been the main antagonist of the concept of general intelligence or *general* convergent ability and has gone to the opposite extreme in fragmenting abilities, recent writers have, on rather weak evidence derived from the use of Guilford's tests, postulated a trait of *general* creativity or *general* divergent thinking.

Divergent thinking, as we have seen, cannot be assumed to be synonymous with creativeness in the '*real world*', although many writers seem to take this as proved (for example, Wallach and Wing 1969). But some connection is plausible (see Dewing 1970 for a little recent positive evidence). The 'divergent-convergent' distinction itself, although very widely used, needs further examination and analysis. The respective tests are usually open-ended versus multiple-choice, the former being appropriate measures of divergent production, which is characterised as the kind of thinking or 'problem-solving' where (unlike convergent thinking) there is no single predetermined correct answer, perhaps even no correct answer; multiple-choice items of the familiar type usually employed in verbal reasoning tests are described as measures of convergent thinking. Item form and psychological process are perhaps being too readily identified. Indeed some 'creativity' tests (such as Mednick's *Remote Associates*), although they are not 'open-ended' but depend upon a predetermined set of right answers, appear to correlate with the open-ended tests and to predict real-life creativity equally well (Shapiro 1968).

Conversely, it is likely that the solution of a difficult 'convergent' problem involves the production of a considerable number of hypotheses before the right one is found, and that good problem-solvers produce more such hypotheses, of more different types, and of more original kinds than other people. In other words, performance on 'convergent' tasks as on 'divergent' could probably be scored for fluency, flexibility and originality (if introspective accounts or other indicators of process were available), the main difference being that a fourth factor is also involved—that of stepping back and seeing whether a hypothesis works or is the best available. An analysis of this kind lends plausibility to Liam Hudson's (1966) hypothesis that scientists are predominantly convergent thinkers and arts specialists predominantly divergent, since the empirical testing of the hypothesis is obviously more vital to scientific than to other kinds of theorising. Cronbach (1968) has argued that the less 'divergent' thinkers are not less fertile in ideas, but that they impose a higher standard of quality control, which may be lowered as anxiety rises.

In the rest of this essay I shall briefly review one or two recent studies, mainly British (since the American literature is so vast and indigestible) concentrating especially on original work that is not readily accessible because reported so far only in theses or other unpublished accounts. Much recent work can be roughly classified as centring on one or more of the following main themes: the relation of creativity or divergent thinking to personality (studies of this type are the least numerous); investigation of Hudson's hypothesis; further exploration of the statistical relation between measures of divergent and convergent thinking (or of 'creativity' and 'intelligence') and of the circumstances in which the two traits are more or less independent, with special reference to the 'threshold' or 'triangular scatterplot' theory.

In connection with the last two questions, many recent workers have suspected that the distinction between convergent and divergent thinking is confounded with or dependent upon a verbalising versus non-verbalising difference, since tests of divergent thinking are predominantly verbal. Thus Christie (1969, page 91) commenting on a study by Hartley and Beasley (1969) at Keele (which had produced results partially confirming the Hudson thesis), writes ' "Meanings for Words" is a test which, in factor analytic studies, consistently shows closer association with verbal intelligence than it does with divergent production. It can be concluded from the Hartley and Beasley study that arts students have greater ability in the verbal domain than science students. That is all.' Similarly Cropley (1968), Fee (1968), Dacey, Madaus and Allen (1969) and Child and Smithers (1971) have all found verbal and non-verbal tests of divergent thinking loading on different factors. Cameron (1968), testing the Hudson hypothesis, or part of it—that divergent thinking would correlate more highly than convergent with performance in English—found the verbal/non-verbal differences more relevant. Verbal tests (whether convergent or divergent) correlated significantly with the criterion, non-verbal (of whichever type) did not. This 'verbal versus non-verbal' distinction is itself obviously in need of refinement. A useful move towards a more precise taxonomy is Birkin's (1970) nine-cell table in which modes of stimulus and response are each classified into 'verbal', 'non-verbal' and 'mixed'. Others have raised similar points and three of the recent researches to be discussed (Nuttall, Mills, Pole) are concerned in greater or lesser degree with the need to separate the convergent-divergent comparison from the verbal/non-verbal and to devise more appropriate measures of scientists' divergent capacity.

Hudson's (arts/diverger versus science/converger) hypothesis is simple and likely but it may be over-simplified and over-stated. Whatever its fate, it has done what any good hypothesis should do—stimulate a lot of interest and further research. In Hudson's approach the study of divergent thinking has fortunately never been encapsulated in any such category as 'cognitive psychology' or 'abilities' but overlaps the field of 'personality study', as is shown by the Joyce and Hudson (1968) paper which suggests that 'divergers' do better from being taught by 'divergers' and 'convergers' by 'convergers'.

Among the few other personality studies, Di Scipio (1968) investigated the relation between divergent/convergent thinking and score on the Eysenck measures of introversion/extraversion. He found the relation to be complex, including different results for males and females and differing effects according as fluency or originality was assessed. Perhaps his most interesting finding was that with verbal IQ partialled out, there was an interaction between introversion/extraversion and neuroticism/stability as predictors of verbal fluency. Stable extraverts were easily the most fluent; neurotic extraverts and neurotic introverts scored almost identically and in the middle range, stable introverts scored lowest. Thus stability co-varied with greater fluency in extraverts but with lesser fluency in introverts. Di Scipio found this interaction however only in males and only when the criterion measure was of simple verbal rather than of ideational fluency. The relation of scores on the latter kind of measure to extroversion and neuroticism was less complex. In males there was a low positive correlation (about $+0.2$) with extraversion, which became somewhat larger with verbal intelligence partialled out. Correlations for females were generally low and non-significant. Di Scipio's research raises at least as many questions as it answers and deserves replication and extension.

Callister (1970) investigated individual differences in preference for complexity or simplicity, using as material randomly generated polygons varying in complexity and also verbal series based on the Miller and Selfridge approximations to natural language. She found a very substantial correlation between the two types of measure and was therefore able to characterise her subjects as preferring a high or low degree of complexity in general.

Her work was based to some degree on that of Munzinger and Kessen and was designed partly to test their hypothesis that preferred level of complexity is a function both of the nature of the material and the coding or data-processing capacity of the individual; but she also included a wide variety of other measures, of intelligence (AH5) of divergent thinking ('uses' test scored for fluency and flexibility), of field dependence, and of personality (Omnibus Personality-Inventory). From the correlations between complexity-preference and these other measures it appeared that the Munzinger-Kessen theory was not supported and that personality factors rather than coding facility were most influential.

In addition, the tests for degree of complexity-preference seemed to provide a valuable indicator of creative temperament in that the 'high complexity preferring' subjects possessed many of the characteristics commonly found in other studies to be associated with creativity, although they were not superior in intelligence. For example they were higher on autonomy, thinking introversion, fluency and flexibility—and the general pattern of validity of the complexity-preference approach was confirmed by the comparison of groups of students specialising in arts subjects, psychology and engineering. Results here varied slightly according to the material employed—verbal or non-verbal—but the descending order in extent of complexity preferred was arts students, psychologists, engineers.

McHenry and Shouksmith (1970) investigated the relation between divergent thinking ability and suggestibility in ten-year-old children. This relation proved to be highly significant; in fact a higher correlation was found between suggestibility and each of the 'creativity' measures than between the separate 'creativity' tests. These results seemed rather para- doxical. It is well known that the work of Mackinnon and of Barron has indicated that, as one might suppose, social conformity (measured, for example, by Asch's techniques) correlates negatively with originality and creativity among individuals (see also Hudson 1968, ch. 2). From the work of Marino (1968, 1971) there are signs that the same is true of national and cultural groups. But an openness to ideas is also a charac- teristic of the creative person, and this openness often approaches gulli- bility. James Strachey has acknowledged a gullibility of this kind in Freud and has claimed that without it his discoveries would not have been possible. The paradox is perhaps more apparent than real, and it may well be that a creative person can be both gullible and non-conformist. Further research on these lines would be welcome.

Shouksmith (1970) summarises the findings contained in five degree theses of Queen's University, Belfast, those of Guy (1965), Irvine (1967), Ledlie (1965), Moore (1966) and Furse-Roberts (1966). Most of these derived from Getzels and Jackson's work (1962) and were concerned with replicating parts of it. The results were rather conflicting, some supporting Getzels and Jackson's findings (e.g. divergent thinking tests independent of convergent and predictive of school achievement), others confirming the presence of a massive general ability factor. Shouksmith also reports a factor analytic study comprising measures of convergent thinking, of divergent thinking, of problem-solving and of cognitive style; one clear conclusion to be drawn from the analysis was 'that males and females do not think alike. Factorially the female group is more complex than the male . . . we see that "creative associating" is opposed to "deductive reasoning" in women, whereas it is not so clearly opposed in men.' Shouksmith links this finding with the existence of fewer women among the ranks of scientists and inventors.

Pole (1969) describes the construction and provisional validation of a new test of creative ability designed for highly intelligent subjects, the initial idea for which originated in a research into factors affecting the career decisions of science students (Hutchings and Pole 1968). There was some suggestion in the findings of the latter research that the *less* creative students were being selected or selecting themselves for postgraduate work in science and in order to test this hypothesis Pole found it desirable if not essential to construct a new test, since she was convinced that most of the existing tests such as those of Guilford and Torrance were likely to appear too trivial to be of interest to university students. In addition a majority of the existing tests, calling principally for a specifically literary creativeness (e.g. 'Word meanings', 'Fables'), were thought likely to penalise and inhibit scientists. On the other hand, existing tests designed to assess scientific ability appeared somewhat cumbersome and tapped mainly convergent ability.

Pole's new test was called *Hypotheses* and consists of a series of statements describing states of affairs for which subjects are asked to provide possible explanations. Two examples are:

1.   Fathers of delinquent children spend more time in public houses than those of non-delinquents.
2.   Two men buy new sets of tyres at the same time; one has to replace his long before the other man's are showing any sign of wear.

The subject is told to suppose each statement to be true, and to give as many possible explanations as he can for each one. Pole claims that this task is at once more challenging and more restricting than those set by most other creativity tests—challenging, because the stimulus has the complexity of a complete situation, rather than being just a single word; and restricting, because all the features in the situation need to be taken into account in producing relevant and plausible responses. Although the test was first conceived as one particularly appropriate for testing science students, the items were not based on specifically scientific material on the ground that, if they had been, the science student might have scored highly as much through scientific knowledge as scientific creativity. As usual with tests of divergent thinking, some problems arose in attempting to devise a relatively objective scoring system. Facetious and 'impossible' answers are disallowed. It would not do, for instance, to provide as an answer to example 2 above the explanation that one man drove his car upside-down.

The *Hypotheses* test had a test-retest reliability of $+0\cdot91$; it related as follows to two more familiar tests of divergent thinking. With Guilford's well known *Uses* test (a version comprising a list of five objects) there was quite a close degree of correspondence in that both *Uses* and *Hypotheses* appeared to measure the same cluster of abilities and to place in a similar order groups of students rated by their tutors as 'seeming to display the most creative ability', 'seeming to display the least creative ability', etc. There was little correspondence however with the other test, which was an adaptation of Hudson's *Meaning of Words*. Pole explains this negative result by interpreting *Meaning of Words* not as a test of divergent thinking, but as a hybrid half-way between that and a conventional intelligence test. This interpretation was based primarily on logical analysis but was supported also by the fact that *Meaning of Words* produced a pattern of results much closer to those from AH5 (a test of convergent thinking) than did either *Uses* or *Hypotheses*. (cf. Christie's evaluation of this test already quoted on page 88.)

Pole's general comments on creativity and intelligence are pleasantly astringent. 'Hudson accused himself of jumping on a bandwagon, but excuses himself with the implication that it is going somewhere and in the right direction. The research reported on in these chapters assesses its passage with greater caution. . . . Creativity is assumed to be a virtue, one best fostered by a "free environment" (meaning America, *circa* 1960), the creative person is more alive, happier, fulfilled. "Intelligence", by contrast, now has a dull and plodding sound; it may be necessary, even desirable, but to cultivate it is narrowing, to rely on it for educational selection and assessment is to promote conformity. This is a bandwagon indeed and one which is out of control.'

Three other recent theses certainly deserve discussion, but for reasons of space can only be briefly mentioned. Ogilvie (1970) investigated divergent thinking in a framework of Piagetian theory; some of his findings supported the 'threshold' or 'triangular scatterplot' hypothesis. Clarke (1968) found that teachers preferred 'convergent' to 'divergent' children (see Getzels and Jackson 1962; Hasan and Butcher 1966), also that their idea of 'creativity' coincided very little with that yielded by the Minnesota battery. Turnbull (1970) investigated originality in children of pre-school age in Aberdeen as related to parental attitude and effect of nursery school.

Nuttall's (1971) work started from some of the same premises as those of Pole; for instance, that existing tests of divergent thinking were generally too heavily loaded with verbal ability and that new tests were required covering a wider range of content. His conclusions, like hers, express some scepticism about inflated claims for tests of divergent thinking. 'The 1960s saw a tremendous surge of interest in divergent thinking tests, which, by 1970, seems out of all proportion to the theoretical and practical significance of the results of studies using such tests.'

Nuttall's battery contained tests of diagrammatic and mathematical divergent thinking either specially constructed or adapted from existing measures including some of the type described by Wood and Skurnik (1969). This is a much-needed development. The current, as yet unpublished, work of Judith Mills at the University of Manchester is also of interest in this connection; her subjects (arts specialists and scientists) themselves implicitly select the mode of response (diagrammatic, symbolic etc.) in which their fluency or originality is to be displayed.

Perhaps the most useful further research in this whole area of divergent thinking would be concerned with set, motivation, testing conditions and the systematic experimental control of all these. What little work has been done so far on these lines has produced interesting hints. Wallach and Kogan (1965) have claimed to show that divergent thinking can be more readily assessed in permissive and non-competitive circumstances. There is some evidence that children of given IQ develop higher divergent ability in 'permissive' than in 'traditional' primary schools (Haddon and Lytton 1968), although no difference was found in a similar study comparing different climates in secondary schools (Lytton and Cotton 1969). Elkind *et al.* (1970) found that children taken from an uninteresting task to do a test of divergent thinking scored very much higher than those taken from an interesting task. Hudson, in *Frames of Mind* describes several very interesting and suggestive small experiments which seem to confirm the special importance of attitude and expectation in this kind of task. It is very likely also that personality differences interact with the circumstances of testing and the type of instruction issued (Boersma and O'Bryan 1968).

Besides aiming to assemble a battery of divergent thinking tests to sample a broader range of content than in most previous researches, Nuttall studied the extent to which divergent thinking tests are likely to be useful in the prediction of scholastic achievement. Since Getzels and Jackson's claim that a group of children scoring highly on tests of divergent thinking had been shown to be the equals scholastically of another (less divergent) group with average IQ 30 points higher, rather little has been demonstrated one way or the other on this issue. Nuttall's study is valuable in that his subjects were sampled so as to represent different types of secondary school and approximately the whole range of ability; he also (and remarkably enough, this technique has rarely been used) examined the predictive validity of divergent thinking measures after that of convergent thinking measures had been allowed for.

As expected, for a particular divergent thinking test (e.g. verbal, diagrammatic) the usual measures of fluency, flexibility and originality generally correlated highly, almost all such correlations being about + 0·7 or higher. The contrast found when one looks at correlations between tests is quite striking. As in other studies there was only a slight degree of correlation between the separate tests of divergent thinking (it made no appreciable difference in this respect whether fluency, flexibility or originality was being compared). Nuttall's research involved two samples, one of secondary school fourth-formers, the other of fifth-formers. The median correlations were respectively + 0·14 and + 0·10.

Both groups of pupils were approximately representative, so far as can be ascertained, of the whole population of such fourth- and fifth-formers; at least no gross restriction of the ability range occurred, though the fifth-form group probably suffered some restriction as compared with the fourth-form owing to selective dropping out of secondary schools. Within the fourth-form sample some detailed analyses were carried out, particularly a comparison of the 'structure of abilities' in the whole group (N = 600+) with that found in grammar school pupils only (N = 100).

Factor analyses in each case included the same thirteen variables (nine convergent measures, including scholastic aptitude tests and tests of spatial and mechanical ability; four divergent). The differences were suggestive, although their statistical significance would be hard to demonstrate. First, only two factors were significant (Guttman's criterion) in the unselected group, but five in the grammar school one. In the total group, it was clear that no factor of divergent thinking emerged; each test of divergent thinking loaded a different factor. The analysis of the grammar school data produced a very different result. In an orthogonal solution, the second factor was clearly interpretable as one of divergent thinking, the three 'established' tests of this type had loadings between 0·64 and 0·78, but of the other ten variables only one loaded over 0·12. An oblique solution produced a closely similar pattern. A third analysis (of the non-grammar school group) produced a pattern of factors and loadings similar to that for the total group. No factor of divergent thinking was perceptible either in the orthogonal or oblique rotated solutions and the tests were dispersed among separate factors.

These clear differences between the factor structure in the grammar school group and that in the total group obviously reflect and summarise differences already present in the respective matrices of inter-correlations. Turning to the most relevant segment of each matrix, we find in the two groups a different relation between performance on the three most typical 'divergent' tests (Tin Can, Squares, Words beginning with TH) and on the two most typical 'convergent' tests (verbal and quantitative sections of a scholastic aptitude test). In the total group, of six correlations *between* the two types of test, all were positive and statistically significant ($p < 0.01$); in the grammar school group, two were negative and of all the positive correlations only one was statistically significant ($p < 0.05$). Just the opposite was true of the correlations *among* the divergent tests, each of these being at least half as large again as in the total group. This greater differentiation of divergent and convergent ability in the more able group (whose mean score was higher on divergent as well as on convergent measures) has been described in some detail because it seems very relevant to the 'threshold' hypothesis, whereby divergent and convergent abilities are more readily distinguishable in high-ability groups.

Although this essay began with some general remarks, it has not been designed to provide a summary of the state of research into divergent thinking and creativity. Its more restricted aim has been to describe a few individual researches, some not readily available in summary, and occasionally to set these descriptions in a rather wider context. But one or two general remarks in conclusion may not be out of place.

The burgeoning of research into creativity has been due in part to a general enthusiasm for 'child-centred' education and to a wave of romantic enthusiasm for the spontaneous. The apparently irrational nature of this enthusiasm has already provoked philosophers into reaction or over-reaction (Peters 1969; White 1968). 'General talk of creativeness is cant' (Peters 1969). Similarly White rules out of court the consideration of creativeness as an inner process.

Psychology could almost be defined as the study of what pundits have proved to be logically incapable of investigation, so we need not be too disturbed by such interdicts. But there is a need for clearer thinking about what is and what is not worth investigation in this field, for the formulation of crucial and testable hypotheses, and for a few large-scale longitudinal and cross-cultural studies. It is appropriate to remind ourselves, in the context of this book as a whole, that the only respectable study of the latter type to be carried out by a psychologist of any nationality is that by Vernon, described in a series of articles listed below in the table of references and summarised in *Intelligence and Cultural Environment* (1969).

H. J. Eysenck

Personality and learning

Early psychometrists have often been accused—not always justly—of giving too much prominence to intelligence generally, and the IQ in particular, when assessing a child's educational potential, or making predictions about a university student's prospects. Intelligence measured by the usual type of intelligence test is certainly important in any kind of scholastic prediction, and the fact that tests for intellectual variables were available, while measures of other variables were not, undoubtedly gave much impetus for the widespread use of IQ tests, and the occasional overemphasis on cognitive factors. Yet such authorities as Sir Cyril Burt and Professor P. E. Vernon have always stressed the importance of personality factors of a non-cognitive kind, and much recent work on the correlation between school success and personality has added emphasis to these adumbrations.

It is not the purpose of this paper to review the voluminous literature which has given some precision to the proposition that personality must be included in any account of the factors predisposing a child (or adolescent) to successful scholastic performance; suffice it to say that two main generalisations seem to result. First, emotionality, anxiety or neuroticism, variously labelled by different investigators, seems to have a negative effect on performance at the primary and secondary school level, with the more emotional or anxious children doing rather worse than the stable ones; at the university level there appears to occur a reversal of this relationship, with the better students having rather high levels of N ('neuroticism'). The reasons for this reversal are unknown, but we shall hazard a guess after we have considered the theoretical conceptions advanced by Spence and other authors. Secondly, introversion seems to favour good performance at the secondary school and the university level; at the primary school level, however, introverts seem to be at a disadvantage.

Eysenck and Cookson (1969), who summarise much of the literature relating to these generalisations, consider that the introvert may correspond to the 'late developer' so often postulated by educationists, but it is also possible that the free-and-easy style of the primary school is better suited to the personality of the extravert, while the introvert gets on better in the more formalised type of education provided by the secondary school, and even better at university. Or possibly the 'late developer' is really an 'early developer' who is disadvantaged at the primary level because of the inappropriately immature level of teaching; it is interesting that Whitlock (1969) found introverts superior to extraverts in a group of very bright primary school children exposed to a rather advanced and more academic teaching programme than is usual.

While it would be wrong to claim that our knowledge in this field is very certain, or that the relations between success and personality are as close and clear-cut as those demonstrated in the ability field, nevertheless there is sufficient evidence already to make it clear that this particular area of research should not be neglected, and that educationalists would be justified in devoting much more research energy to the unravelling of the connections between educational success and personality than they have done in the past. Investigations in the past have usually been *ad hoc* and rather unsystematic; for the greater part, investigators have rested content with simple descriptive statistics, such as correlations, gathered without special concern for various parameters of crucial importance, which ought to have been controlled, or at least measured. Such control is of course only possible when some reasonable hypotheses already exist in a given field; research not based on such hypotheses is not likely to advance our knowledge very much. It is for this reason that I have concentrated in this chapter on a survey of data related to a theory linking personality and learning. While far from complete, or able to account for all the empirical findings, this theory nevertheless has been able to make large numbers of testable predictions, many of which have been verified. Much of this work stems from the laboratory, rather than from the classroom, but this does not mean that the results of such work as here summarised are not relevant to classroom practices. The failure of educational empiricism and academic theorising to come together has always been one of the more distressing features of the educational scene; this chapter attempts to make a small move in the direction of such reconciliation.

The theory in question is Spence's adaptation of Hull's general learning theory; a good statement of the theory, together with a survey of the evidence, is given in a recent paper by Spence and Spence (1966), and a rather more extensive review is given by Eysenck (1971). Taking into account only the most relevant concepts, we might simplify this theory by saying that $D \times H = P$, i.e. performance on a given task is a product of motivation (drive, D) and learning (habit, H). All these constructs are

D

of course carefully defined in the Hullian system, and many others are introduced to take into account such factors as behavioural oscillation, reactive inhibition, and threshold levels; nevertheless, for our present purpose these must be neglected.

It may also be noted that theoreticians of widely different plumage have adopted rather similar formulae; Tolman, in many ways an out-spoken critic of Hull's system, nevertheless comes to much the same con-clusion (McCorquodale and Meehl 1954). Spence now proposes to use this theory in order to bring personality into the Hullian formulation; his suggestion is that *anxiety acts like a drive*, so that persons who are charac-terised by strong anxiety are in fact in a state of high drive. (In Hull's system all drives summate to bring about the final drive state, D; this enables Spence to add anxiety to whatever other drives may be active in a given situation.) For the measurement of anxiety Spence habitually uses the Manifest Anxiety Scale (MAS), a conglomerate of anxiety-related statements from the Minnesota Multiphasic Personality Inventory (MMPI).

In his earliest work, Spence made predictions from his theory in relation to eyeblink conditioning; his argument was that in this situation, where a tone constituted the conditioned stimulus (CS) and a puff of air to the cornea the unconditioned stimulus (UCS), there would be no pre-existing habits to interfere with the simple establishment of a connection, through experimental pairing of the CS and the UCS, resulting in eye-blink when the tone was sounded. This being so, and all subjects starting out from a habit strength of zero, subjects with higher drive (high anxiety) should develop the conditioned response (closure of the eye) more rapidly than subjects with lower drive (little anxiety). The experi-mental literature supports this prediction with some regularity, although results may be negative when the conditions of the experiments are not made anxiety-provoking enough, e.g. through the provision of visual stimuli, such as electric apparatus, which may suggest shock and other fear-producing effects.

When we come to the learning of verbal material, or other complex matters, the assumption of zero habit strength can no longer be made, and Spence's theory becomes more involved. Suppose the subject of our experiment is required to learn the paired-associate item: Table—Fish. Clearly there are already in existence many other associations, such as Table—Chair, which have a fair degree of habit strength; the to-be-acquired association has to compete with these older ones. Drive multiplies impartially with existing habits, and if the to-be-learned habit has to compete with older established ones, then it will be the more difficult to learn, the higher the drive—for the simple reason that the high drive multiplies with the existing habit (which has high habit strength) and thus produces a strong performance potential. Unfortunately for the learner, of course, this performance potential is for the wrong (old-established) association; consequently he will find it all the more difficult to learn the new association, the higher his drive! Thus in complex learning, Spence makes predictions which depend on the strength of existing habits, as well as on the degree of drive; these existing habits may either be learned during the experimental session, which brings them under proper experimental control, or else they may have been acquired during the subject's past life, like the association between Table and Chair.

Spence would thus predict that new associations competing with older ones would be established more quickly in low anxiety subjects, because in these the older associations would have little performance potential because of the low drive. Gradually, however, this position would change as the new associations were in fact learned, and once their habit strength surpassed that of the older associations, they would be learned better by the high drive subjects. These predictions, and this analysis, are both clearly relevant to school learning, and it should be added that they may also be relevant to educational practices in other ways than simply in relation to personality differences; high-anxiety drive can be induced even in low-anxiety subjects by threats, by punishment, or by other manipulations of the situation in which the child finds himself. Thus a low-anxiety boy or girl in a high-anxiety situation may behave like a high-anxiety child in a situation not itself highly productive of anxiety; in this way the educationalist can manipulate the environment to produce complex interactions with personality and performance.

Spence's theoretical account has been firmly related to the empirical side by a lengthy series of experimental studies. One of his first attempts to provide empirical content for his theories was in relation to serial maze learning; he assumed that at many choice points anticipatory or perseverative tendencies would be present to such a degree that the incorrect choice would be stronger than the correct one. It was therefore predicted that high-anxiety subjects would show a greater number of errors on the learning trials than low-anxiety subjects; he also expected to find a correlation between the rank order of the 'difficulty' of the choice points (as indexed by the total number of errors made on each) and the magnitude of the difference between the errors made by high-anxiety and low-anxiety groups. Farber and Spence (1953), Taylor and Spence (1952), Matarazzo, Ulett and Saslow (1955), Axelrod, Cowen and Heilitzer (1956) have confirmed one or other of these predictions; Hughes, Sprague and Bendig (1954) confirmed neither. In another series of studies, Spence employed serial learning tasks in which subjects were presented with successive items and required to anticipate the next item on the list. Lucas (1952) and Montague (1953) showed that the differences between the overall performance of high- and low-anxiety groups increased in favour of the latter in conformity with intralist similarity and intralist competition. Similarly, on a serial rote learning task, Malmo and Amsel (1948) found anxious patients to make more errors than normals.

For various theoretical reasons, Spence gave up work on serial learning (Spence and Spence 1966) and concentrated rather on paired-associate learning, using non-competitive lists, i.e. lists containing a minimum of previously established associations. Prediction of quicker progress of high-anxiety groups was verified by Spence (1958), Taylor (1958) and Taylor and Chapman (1955), but not by Kamin and Fedorchak (1957) and Lovaas (1960). More consistently favourable have been results in experiments where the to-be-learned associations were already present in the minds of the subjects (e.g. Table—Chair); here high-anxiety subjects should do better. Besch (1959), Spence, Farber and McFann (1956), Spence, Taylor and Ketchel (1956), and Standish and Champion (1960), have provided confirmatory evidence on this point. The obverse of this prediction is of course that when the established associations are different from the to-be-learned ones, then low-anxiety subjects would be superior; Ramond (1953), the two Spence *et al.* studies already cited, and the Standish and Champion (1960) report have provided evidence in favour of this prediction. Spielberger and Smith (1966) too, may be quoted in support; they also showed that personality and test conditions interact, by demonstrating that the predicted differences between high- and low-anxiety subjects were only found under stressful conditions, not when stress was not present. Castaneda and Palermo (1955) provide a similar demonstration. Katahn (1964) and Katahn and Lyda (1966) verified results reported by Standish and Champion; they had subjects first learn a highly dominant response word to the stimulus word, then had the same subjects learn a non-dominant response word to the same stimulus word. High-anxiety subjects learned the dominant word more readily, low-anxiety subjects the non-dominant word.

Work with children has been particularly concerned with the interaction between drive level and degree of intratask competition; using motor learning tasks, Castaneda and his co-workers used a children's version of the Manifest Anxiety Scale (MAS) or manipulated the drive variable by means of time stress (Castaneda 1956, 1961; Castaneda,

Palermo and McCandless 1956; Castaneda and Lipsitt 1959; see also Clark 1962). These studies have given predominantly positive results. Altogether, the outcome of the studies surveyed (and many others not cited) has on the whole been favourable to the theory put forward by Spence; however, some results have suggested the need for an extension of the theory, by taking into account the importance of drive stimuli (S_D). The inclusion of this concept in the system necessitates a brief theoretical retake.

Hull's system relies very much on primary drives (hunger, thirst, sex) and the reinforcement provided by drive-reduction (eating, drinking, intercourse); he also, however, postulates secondary drives and secondary reinforcements. Anxiety, on this view, is a term denotative of a secondary drive, and also a source of secondary reinforcement. As Hilgard (1956) puts it, 'the primary drive involved in this case is pain; neutral stimuli associated with pain give rise to "fear" responses, very similar to responses to pain, and the proprioceptive consequences of these learned responses produce the drive stimulus (S_D) that serves the secondary drive'.

This conditioned fear response is the psychologist's conception of 'anxiety'; the diminution of anxiety has the properties of reinforcement, and hence can serve to cause learning. Anxiety may be unique in having both these functions; few other examples come to mind of secondary *drives*, although there are many studies using secondary *reinforcers* (Cravens and Renner, 1970). Tokens which may be exchanged for food will act as secondary reinforcers for hungry chimps, but they will only cause him to work when hungry (primary drive). Miller (1948, 1951), in a series of classical studies, showed, first, that neutral stimuli became fear arousing after association with noxious stimuli, and could serve as the basis for motivating an animal in a learning situation so that it strove to escape; and second, that reduction of the fear through cessation of the conditioned fear stimulus constituted a reinforcing event in that it led to the learning of the responses which it followed.

Drive stimuli are proprioceptive stimuli produced by the conditioned fear responses; in humans they are capable of being verbalised (introspected), and consist of such reactions as rapid heart beat, rapid breathing, blushing or blanching, muscular innervation, 'feeling sick', and in extreme cases micturition or even defecation. Other drive stimuli are associated with hunger or thirst, or with sexual deprivation; these are too well known to require description. Drive stimuli can become very strong, and may generate task-irrelevant behaviour which may interfere with the behaviour to be learned. 'The extensions of our notions concerning drive and anxiety involved what might be called the "response interference hypothesis", the hypothesis that states that task-irrelevant

responses which in some situations may interfere with efficient performance are more easily elicited in high than in low anxiety subjects' (Spence
and Spence 1966).

What Spence is telling us here is (a) that previously existing and
competing habits are not the only handicap which retards efficient
earning, but that drive stimuli may also be a nuisance by generating task-
interfering behaviour—such as worrying about the result of an examination rather than getting on with it, or withdrawing from the anxiety-
generating situation, or thinking that one might be suffering from a
cardiac dysfunction. He also maintains (b) that high-anxiety subjects are
more prone to suffer from these interfering effects of the S_D, presumably
because the D is so much stronger in them. This additional source of
interference in high-anxiety subjects did not form part of Spence's original
theory; it was incorporated in order to accommodate some criticisms
presented by Child (1954), and the results of experimental studies which
could not be explained simply in terms of the original theory. It should be
noted that like D, so S_D may help or hinder performance, depending upon
whether the response tendencies instigated by S_D are compatible with the
task to be performed, or not (Amsel 1950; Amsel and Maltzman 1950).

Spence and his associates have used three main types of anxiety-
provoking situations. One was the use of ego-involving instructions, i.e.
instructions suggesting that success in the experimental task had a bearing
on the subject's IQ, his personality, or his scholastic standing (Nicholson
1958; Sarason 1957a, b; Katchmar, Ross and Andrews 1958; Sarason 1961;
Sarason and Palola 1960). A second was the use of failure experiences as a
means of inducing stress (Sarason 1956; Gordon and Berlyne 1954;
Lucas 1952; Sarason 1957b; Katchmar, Ross and Andrews 1958, and
Taylor 1958). A third was the use of noxious stimulation, usually shock
(Besch 1959; Chiles 1958; Lee 1961; Deese, Lazarus and Keenan 1953;
Lazarus, Deese and Hamilton 1954; Silverman and Blitz 1956; Davidson,
Andrews and Ross 1956). With the exception of the work using shock,
which is very contradictory, the results were on the whole in line with
hypothesis. The importance of S_D seems as firmly established as the
relevance of D (anxiety) in the pathology of learning.

The potential applications of these theories to educational, clinical
and other applied uses are obvious, although, as Spence and Spence (1966)
recognise, 'whether these results can be generalised to other measures of
manifest anxiety, e.g., clinical judgements, will require empirical demonstration'. However that may be, there can be little doubt that Spence
has made a major contribution to this field; nevertheless, there are a
number of points on which he may be (and has been) criticised. Thus, use

of the MAS has been criticised because it does not correlate at all well with physiological measures of emotional arousal or drive, which are believed to have greater validity and to be more fundamental, and it has been suggested that such physiological measures should be employed by preference instead of the MAS.

Spence and Spence (1966) refute this criticism by arguing that 'in the Hull-Spence system . . . the drive concept is purely mathematical in nature, being defined in terms of observable manipulations and related mathematically to other similarly defined concepts, deductions from the entire theoretical network permitting predictions to be made about behaviour. Since the concepts in this behavioural system are convenient mathematical fictions rather than speculations about physiological facts, it is totally inappropriate to refer, literally, to "measuring" drive and thus to compare the directness, purity, or whatever of various methods of defining the concept.' The purity of this method of working with mathematical concepts, and the operational definition given in terms of the MAS, make argument difficult; scientific discussion about empirical facts dissolves into philosophical speculation about optimal research strategies. However that may be, the Spence position seems very dated now, and his adoption of the 'empty organism' or black box as the abode of these mathematical fictions fails to take into account advances in physiological research which may with advantage be taken into account in constructing theories in this field.

Possibly even more important as a source of confusion is Spence's failure to take into account the fact that the MAS is not a univocal measure of a single dimension of personality; it has been shown to be highly correlated with N (Neuroticism) and somewhat less highly with E (Extraversion) (negatively). These correlations are sufficiently high to indicate that all the variance of the MAS is in fact accounted for by these two personality dimensions. High MAS scorers are thus dysthymics, or introverted high-N scorers. In assessing the many studies summarised in the preceding paragraphs it is clearly impossible to answer the important question of whether the differences between high- and low-scoring subjects on the MAS are due to differences in N, differences in E, or both. Thus interpretation is impeded on what is really a crucial point, and further development hindered (Eysenck and Eysenck 1969). As we shall see, the problems raised are quite important, and the writer's own theory, while using Spence's concept of anxiety as a drive, has developed along somewhat different lines, using both physiological hypotheses and more clearly univocal personality measures, such as the Maudsley Personality Inventory (MPI) and the Eysenck Personality Inventory (EPI).

Eysenck's attempts to link personality theory with learning and conditioning phenomena had its origin in the personality field itself (Eysenck 1957, 1967). In this primary orientation it differs from that of Spence and Spence (1966) who point out that 'the interests of those of us who developed and first used the (MAS) scale can be described as being both broader and narrower than anxiety as a personality characteristic, the studies growing out of a series of investigations that have been concerned with the role of aversive motivational or drive factors in learning situations, primarily classical conditioning, with the framework of Hull-Spence behaviour theory'. The starting point of Eysenck's series of studies, *per contra*, was the discovery that individual differences in behaviour, whether in the laboratory or in life, could be described in considerable detail in terms of two major personality dimensions, extraversion and neuroticism (Eysenck and Eysenck 1969). These individual differences could be shown to be firmly anchored in heredity, and certain hypotheses were finally put forward relating neuroticism to the lability of the autonomic system and the visceral brain, extraversion to differing thresholds in the reticular formation–cortex arousal loop (Eysenck 1967).

Thus high-N scorers are seen as over-reactors to emotional stimuli, whether these are conditioned or unconditioned; introverts are seen as having high cortical levels of arousal. This split in the unitary conception of the 'activating' as opposed to the 'directing' aspect of human behaviour is of considerable importance; corresponding to it we have a possible association between Hullian 'drive' and cortical arousal (an identification adumbrated by Hebb), and the possibility that S_D might be more closely associated with the visceral brain-autonomic system loop. Eysenck (1967) also points out that these two systems are not independent; high emotional activation produces cortical arousal both through direct connections between hypothalamus and cortex and through interoceptive stimuli activating the reticular formation (see figure 1). In this theory, then, we would tentatively identify Spence's D with cortical arousal, and on the personality side with introversion; on this interpretation, then, the causal factor in the relations established by Spence between anxiety and learning would be borne by the introversion component, not the N component.

Some supportive evidence on this point is available from a study by Willoughby (1967), who repeated the Spence, Farber and McFann (1956) study on the relation between anxiety and performance level in competitive and non-competitive paired-associate learning; however, instead of using the MAS, with its 'contamination' of introversion, he used a pure measure of N or emotionality. He found the high-N subjects inferior to low-N subjects on the competitive paired-associates list, as expected on

Spence's hypothesis; he also found high-N subjects inferior on the non-competitive list, which is clearly contrary to Spence's hypothesis. As he points out, 'one possible basis for the discrepancy is that the "introversion" component is the main factor in the MAS producing a performance differential on the non-competitive pairs'. It seems likely that the guilty

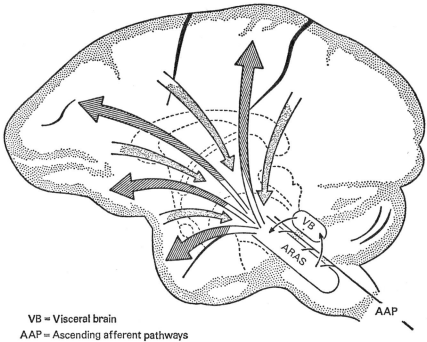

VB = Visceral brain
AAP = Ascending afferent pathways
ARAS = Ascending reticular activating system

FIGURE I   *Diagrammatic representation of personality correlates at the physiological level. Neuroticism is hypothesised to be associated with individual differences in reactivity of the visceral brain and the autonomic system; extraversion is hypothesised to be associated with cortical arousal differences mediated by the reticular formation.*

party responsible for this effect was the S$_D$ produced in susceptible (high-N) subjects by the testing situation. Willoughby also reported similar findings with eyeblink conditioning. It is unfortunate that with this one exception, studies of the Spence type have never used inventories measuring both N and E; our understanding of the dynamics of learning in relation to personality would be much further advanced than they are in fact, had they done so.

The type of prediction mediated by the writer's theories has a certain paradoxical air, due to complications which arise from well-established experimental demonstrations. At first sight, one might be inclined to feel that introverts, characterised by high arousal, would obviously be superior in learning and remembering, and also in reminiscence. (Reminiscence is the technical name given to the phenomenon of improvement in performance during a rest pause following massed practice.) This prediction is indeed correct, but its verification is complicated by certain details of the physiological processes accompanying and underlying learning. According to the latest theory (John 1967), the process of consolidation of the memory trace is of fundamental importance in all learning, and it in turn is profoundly influenced by the degree of cortical arousal obtaining at the time; the greater the degree of arousal, the stronger and more prolonged the consolidation process, and consequently the greater the permanence and accessibility of the memory traces laid down.

To these postulates, which essentially govern the transformation of short-term memory, conceptualised as a set of reverberating neural circuits, into long-term memory, conceptualised as a permanent chemical transformation of the cell material through some form of protein synthesis, must be added certain others (Walker 1958; Walker and Tarte 1963) concerned with what these authors call *action decrement*. As they point out, 'during the active period (of consolidation), there is a degree of temporary inhibition to recall, i.e. action decrement (this negative bias against repetition serves to protect the consolidating trace against disruption). High arousal during the associative process will result in a more intensely active trace process. The more intense activity will result in greater ultimate memory but greater temporary inhibition against recall.' According to this theory we would therefore expect that extraverts, having low arousal and weak consolidation, would actually show better recall soon after learning, because in introverts the continuing consolidation process would interfere with recall; it would only be later on, when consolidation had ceased, that introverts would appear superior. What is predicted, therefore, is a cross-over effect, with extraverts demonstrating forgetting, and introverts reminiscence (improvement over time).

Several investigations are available to support the first part of the hypothesis, i.e. that linking extraversion to superior learning and memory ability when the interval between learning and recall is short (Jensen 1962; Howarth 1963; Shanmugan and Santhanam 1964; Jensen 1964; Siegman 1957; Gebhardt 1966; Howarth 1969a, 1969b). Results are remarkably unanimous, and have been reviewed in detail by Eysenck (1971). The only exception is a study by Grant (1969), which is of considerable interest because here, for reasons to be given presently, the experimental design is such as to make one predict that introverts would in fact be superior. He presented a series of forty-eight items to each subject, consisting of twenty-four 3-letter words and twenty-four 3-letter trigrams; each was singly presented and tested for recall. Eight items were

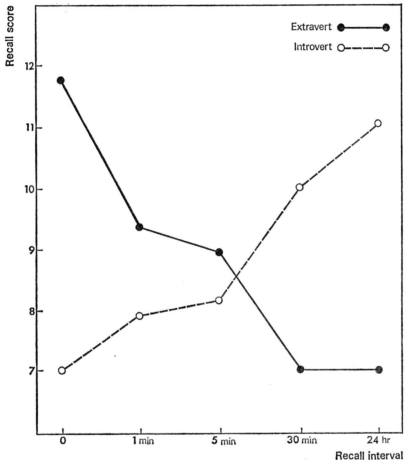

FIGURE 2 *Cross-over effect in recall for paired-associate learning after different intervals; introverts show reminiscence, extraverts show forgetting.*

tested after each of six different retention intervals (3, 6, 9, 12, 15 and 18 seconds). The retention interval was filled with counting backwards by threes or fours from a 3-digit number. It is well known that under these conditions most forgetting takes place with the first three seconds (Talland 1967; Dillon and Reid 1969). This suggests that consolidation of the memory trace (which is of course a very simple one in this case, being made up of only one single word or trigram) is by then almost complete. If this were so, then no competition of the consolidation process with recall would take place, and the amount recalled would be a direct function of the amount of arousal; hence one might expect on our hypothesis that introverts would recall more—which they do.

A proper demonstration of the cross-over phenomenon was given by Howarth and Eysenck (1968), in an experiment specially designed to test this hypothesis. From over 600 students, 110 were selected on the basis of their EPI scores as being extraverted or introverted, and having relatively low N scores. Seven pairs of Complex Verbal Coding tasks (cvc) of medium association value were used in four orders of presentation; the criterion of learning was that the correct response should be given to each item of the list during one consecutive presentation. The subsequent retention interval (up to 30 minutes) was occupied with the subject making up words out of a longer word. Recall intervals of 0, 1 min., 5 mins., 30 mins., or 24 hours were used with different groups of subjects, and a highly significant interaction between extraversion and recall interval was observed. Results are shown in figure 2; as predicted, extraverts have superior recall after short intervals, and inferior recall after long intervals.

A rather different approach to the study of personality-learning interaction to that described above was undertaken by McLaughlin and Eysenck (1967). This study was based on the hypothesis that the four personality groups (E+ N+, E+ N−, E− N+ and E− N−) can be arranged along a continuum of arousal, from the lowest (E+ N−) to the highest (E− N+), with the other two intermediate. On the basis of the Yerkes-Dodson law (also sometimes called the inverted-U relation between drive and performance), performance on a paired-associates nonsense syllable learning task should show the usual inverted-U shape when plotted on this continuum; for a difficult task the optimum point of this inverted-U should be shifted towards the low arousal side.

Two lists were constructed to meet the requirements of having stimulus members of high meaningfulness, low similarity and response members of intermediate meaningfulness and either high similarity or low similarity. Stimulus and response members of low similarity had a minimal number of letters in common, while the responses of high similarity all had the same vowel and one consonant in common. In all pairs similarity between stimuli and responses was minimised as much as possible. Sixty-four subjects were assigned to one of the personality groups; eight members of each group were given the easy list, the other eight the difficult list. Results are shown in figure 3; extraverts perform better throughout, which is in line with expectation, as testing immediately followed

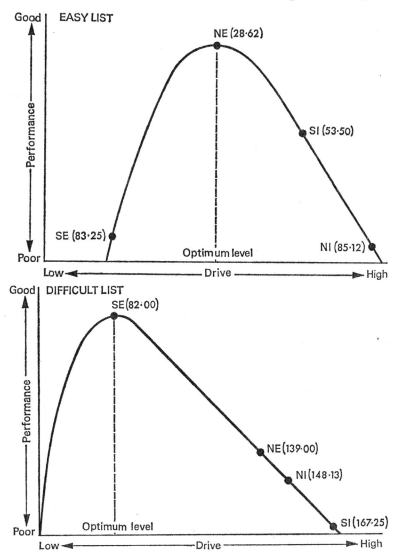

FIGURE 3   *Performance of different personality types (stable extraverts, stable introverts, neurotic extraverts, neurotic introverts) on easy and difficult list (paired-associate learning). Note that the stable extravert group actually performs better on the difficult list, as compared with the easy list.*

learning, and consolidation would thus have the maximal interfering effect on the introverts. Of greater interest is the fact that the second order interaction (E× N× difficulty) is also significant beyond the 1 per cent level; this is direct support for our hypothesis.

A very carefully controlled experiment by McLean (1968) must be mentioned to round off this brief survey of relevant work; it is too extensive to be described in detail, but essentially McLean controlled, in addition to personality variable (through selection on the basis of EPI scores), by measuring within-subject arousal (through the use of psychophysical measures), and by imposing low arousal or high arousal conditions (through the use of white noise in order to induce high arousal). He also compared incidental and intentional learning, using paired-associate learning of single digits paired with nonsense syllables. The result which is of main interest here is that 'extraverts performed better than introverts on immediate (2 minutes) paired-associate recall tests, but introverts performed better than extraverts on delayed (24 hours) recall tests. The interaction between extraversion and recall interval was . . . statistically significant ($p < 0.01$).' This experiment, taken together with the Howarth and Eysenck one, gives strong support to the chain of hypotheses and predictions described in this chapter; it is because the cross-over effect is such an unexpected one to emerge on any other hypothesis that it supports the present theory so strongly.

It is difficult to summarise the large body of work referred to in this chapter, but certain important conclusions may perhaps be pointed out with some advantage. The first point which emerges with absolute clarity is that personality and learning interact; it should be clear that the comparative neglect into which personality variables have fallen when research designs were being discussed is not only undeserved and unnecessary, but also inimical to successful and meaningful work. Frequently different personality types or groups show *opposite* effects to each other when certain parameters in the experimental design are being altered; if no information is being collected on personality types, then these meaningful differences merely serve to increase the size of the error term. It has often been remarked that verbal reminiscence is a 'now you see it, now you don't' phenomenon, and work on it has practically ceased for this reason. The data summarised in figure 2 show that over time introverts show reminiscence, extraverts forgetting; average the two, and you get no effect at all! The inclusion of personality variables in studies of this type is not only desirable, but completely essential; without them, no meaningful replicable results can be expected.

The second point to be noted is that theories exist which can mediate and predict many of the empirical observations. It is not necessary to claim that these theories have reached a very high level of sophistication, or are able to handle all the data available. Clearly there are still many complexities in this field which call for improvements in the available theories, and some results which are difficult to explain even now. But on the whole the predictions made by Spence and by the writer have been verified so many times that it would not be correct to say that our theories are help-less in the face of the complexity of the data; clearly there must be some-thing true and correct in these theories, even though in part they may still be in need of improvement. It must also be borne in mind that only very few people have in fact taken part in this work; most of it has been done by Spence and his associates and students, or by the writer and the Maudsley group. Great improvements may be expected when a more general search for more inclusive principles is carried out by a larger body of people.

The third point relates to application of these theories and relations to educational practice. This may either be direct, i.e. making deductions from the theories themselves as they stand, or indirect, i.e. by taking a rather wider view of the theoretical framework. Consider the fact that, as mentioned in the introductory paragraph, high-N scorers seem to do rather poorly in primary and secondary school, but rather better than average at university. Our theory suggests an answer. High-N scorers have strong S_D to contend with; university students may have learned to use these constructively, i.e. in ways which are compatible with scholastic success, while schoolboys would still react in ways which are incompatible with success. Thus a student high on N might react to strong anxiety prior to an examination by working extra hard; this would be compatible anxiety-induced behaviour leading to success; anxiety would thus be acting as a secondary drive in the right direction. Another student might be led by his strong anxiety, and the accompanying S_D, to get drunk, or seek solace in feminine company; this would be conduct incompatible with success. Similarly, a schoolboy might develop a school phobia under similar conditions, or might be so worried that he suffered from 'examina-tion fright', and was unable to do himself justice. It seems likely that experience over the years would lead students to a point where appropriate reactions to the S_D would be more common; it also seems likely that those whose school experiences did not lead to such appropriate reactions would be 'selected against', and never reach the university.

These considerations (which are, of course, speculative—there is no direct evidence to show that this explanation is in fact the correct one for the facts of differential correlation between N and scholastic success at school and at university) suggest that knowledge of the child's N score might be of great help to the teacher in dealing with problems of anxiety and under-achievement, and might even suggest ways and means of turning the negative influence of high N into a positive drive leading rather to over-achievement. Similarly, differences in E may lead to differential response of children to different types of teaching; the superiority of extraverts in primary school, and of introverts in secondary school, has already been mentioned, and so has the theory that this may be linked with different types of teaching. By suitable adaptation of teaching methods, the introvert might be helped at the primary school level, the extravert at secondary school level.

Specific suggestions about methods of teaching suitable for different personality types must of course draw upon a broader basis than that offered in these brief notes; in fact, research in this field is unfortunately almost completely lacking. It is not impossible to make certain suggestions based on fairly well-established evidence; thus the rapid onset of inhibition, and the lack of vigilance, which characterise extraverts by virtue of their low arousal, suggest that for them teaching should be broken up into many self-contained small 'parcels', with rest-pauses in between, while for introverts longer, more continuous teaching is advantageous. Similarly, the use of devices to break up the monotony will be much more urgently needed when teaching extraverts than when teaching introverts. The highly interpersonal needs of the extraverts suggest that machine teaching would be more successful with introverts, and the evidence suggests that this is indeed so (Eysenck 1967).

Clearly the tail end of a chapter on personality and learning is not the right place to embark on a detailed account of the possible ways and means of gearing teaching to the personality of the pupils in question; in any case serious attempt to do so would need the co-operation of teachers and psychologists. The few suggestions outlined above are only meant to serve as a reminder that the theoretical and experimental studies here reviewed have certain applied consequences which may be very practical indeed; it is to be hoped that educationalists will in the future pay more attention than they have done in the past to the importance of personality theory in dealing with the problems arising in the classroom. The search for a 'best' method of teaching is clearly futile; methods are optimal only when they respond to the very different needs and drives of different children, and research is only likely to be successful if it is based on a scientific understanding of just what these needs and drives are. Spence has pioneered a way into this complex and difficult field; even though his theories may be on the way to being superseded, he should nevertheless be remembered as an innovator whose contribution will prove of very great value indeed.

J. Kane

Mental and personality correlates of motor abilities

The concept of integrated development as recently proposed by Cowell and France (1963) and Ismail and Gruber (1967), goes beyond the speculative philosophies of body-mind interaction and interdependence. Their purpose is to provide in a systematic way continuing research evidence to support their views of the integrated nature of man's development and abilities. As a beginning they have concerned themselves with the relationship between motor and intellectual performances and have now provided probably the first experimental evidence of the nature and extent of this relationship. The notion that in his development and in the expression of his abilities man constantly demonstrates the interrelationship between his physical, social, emotional and intellectual resources is not new. Rousseau (see Van Dalen 1953) has been credited with being among the earliest educational theorists to appreciate fully this point. More recently the physiologist Sherrington (1940) emphasised in particular the link between the mind and the motor act in suggesting that 'the muscle is the cradle of the recognisable mind', and that human thinking and imagery is only communicable through movement—in speech, writing, playing, gesture and other forms of motor acts. Sherrington wrote: '. . . mind, recognisable mind, seems to have arisen in connection with the motor act. Where motor integration progressed and where motor behaviour progressively evolved, mind progressively evolved.' Straus (1968) in his philosophical treatment of the upright posture also refers to the essential integration of mind and body movement. He contends that the process of learning movements is governed by the appreciation of the anticipated movements in its entirety. There must exist, apparently, a mental image of the acceptable level of the motor function and our patterns of movement are regulated by the concept of the finished performance imprinted on the brain.

The interdependence of the psyche and the soma has the additional support of modern medical science. Although much remains to be learnt about the integrative function of the central nervous system, neurologists are agreed about psychosomatic interaction and acknowledge its significance in the full understanding of man's behaviour.

In the field of education, none are more sensitive than physical educationists of the way in which behaviour and performance may be linked with functions of the mind and personality. Their work requires them to be specially aware of the sensory processes associated with the perception and transmission of information to the central nervous system for analysis, synthesis and the integrative regulation which results in co-ordinated movement. It is not surprising, therefore, that they have always strongly attested to their belief in the concept of the mind-body relationship. They have for long considered that physical abilities constitute an important link in the structure of human abilities and that they represent vital aspects in the process of integrated development and adjustment. The research evidence in support of these contentions has not been substantial and has been mostly indirect and inferential.

Motor and intellectual performance

The recent work of Cowell, Ismail and their colleagues is therefore of particular value. Confining themselves particularly to one aspect of the functional relationship between body and mind, namely, to the nature and extent of the association between motor and intellectual performances, they have provided some hard experimental evidence to support their broad based theory of integrated development. Up to this point in time most researchers in this area had reported only low and insignificant correlation between mental abilities and physical measures such as physique, dental age, height, weight, grip strength and power (e.g. Bloomers *et al.* 1955; Klausmeier *et al.* 1959). The erroneous general conclusion was that there was little or no relationship between mental and motor performance.

In 1963, however, Ismail, Kephart and Cowell found that neuro-muscular coordination items as well as static and dynamic balance items were substantially present in an academic development factor which they identified. From this starting point Ismail and Gruber (1965) undertook a series of sequential studies on fifth and sixth grade children. Forty-two measures of physical and intellectual abilities were collected and inter-correlated. The following is a summary of the findings from these investigations:

1. Growth measures (i.e. height and weight) are not significantly related to either IQ or academic achievement.

2.   Measures of strength, speed, power and accuracy are virtually un-related to IQ or academic achievement.

3.   Measures of coordination (e.g. various hopping patterns on one or both feet) are positively related to IQ and academic achievement. Correlation coefficients tend to be in the moderate range.

4.   Balance and kinaesthetic skills are positively related to IQ and academic achievement. Correlation coefficients tend to be moderate to low.

5.   The pattern of correlations tends to be the same for boys and girls.

6.   The pattern of correlations tends to differ somewhat for groups of high, middle and low achievers.

The correlation matrices for the total group, for boys and for girls, were separately submitted to factor analysis and in each case the largest factor extracted was named *Academic Development* because of high loadings on IQ and academic achievement test items. However, this factor was consistently found to have moderate loadings on coordination and balance items indicating that these aspects of motor aptitude are linked with academic achievement (table 1). A further extension of these analyses showed that it was possible to compute satisfactory regression equations for the prediction of academic achievement from motor aptitude tests. Multiple correlations ranged from 0·92 to 0·62 for groups of boys and girls who were high, medium or low achievers (Ismail and Gruber 1965). The motor tests having the highest predictive value were coordination and balance items and those having a negligible value were measures of speed, power and strength.

Recent support for these findings has come from Yoder (1968) and Kirkendall (1968). Not only did Kirkendall find among fifth and sixth graders an Academic Development factor with moderately high loading on lower limb coordination and balance, but he demonstrated that upper limb coordination items discriminated between high, medium and low achievers. Cross cultural validation has also been provided. British primary school eleven-year-old boys and girls were given tests of motor and intellectual capacity which closely approximated to those used earlier in the USA by Ismail. The results of this British study (Ismail, Kane and Kirkendall 1969) were in general strikingly similar to those in which the subjects had been American children. In particular the Academic Development factor identified in this study was almost identical in pattern and loadings to the one described for the American sample in which the co-ordination and balance items were substantially present.

TABLE I   *Summary of factor analytic studies depicting the rotated factor loadings coordination items on an Academic Development factor*

Ismail and Gruber (1967), 5th and 6th grade children, N = 211

Total group		Boys		Girls	
Hop 2 right & 2 left	0·33	Hop 2 right & 2 left	0·27	Age	−0·32
Hop 2 left & 2 right	0·35	Hop 2 left & 2 right	0·36	Hop right & left	0·28
Hop 2 right & 1 left	0·53	Hop 2 right & 1 left	0·34	Hop 2 right & 2 left	0·38
Hop 2 left & 1 right	0·39	Hop 2 left & 1 right	0·22	Hop 2 left & 2 right	0·60
IQ	0·90	IQ	0·83	Hop 2 left & 1 right	0·51
Paragraph meaning	0·91	Paragraph meaning	0·92	IQ	0·92
Word meaning	0·92	Word meaning	0·91	Paragraph meaning	0·91
Arith. reasoning	0·90	Arith. reasoning	0·91	Word meaning	0·93
Arith. computation	0·79	Arith. computation	0·81	Arith. reasoning	0·91
Total Stanford Achiev.	0·96	Total Stanford Achiev.	0·98	Arith. computation	0·86
				Total Stanford Achiev.	0·96

Ismail, Kane and Kirkendall (1969), English primary school children, N = 130

Total group		Boys		Girls	
Hop left foot	0·21	Hop left foot	0·28	Hop left & right	0·31
Hop left & right	0·22	Hop 1 right & 2 left	0·26	Hop 1 left & 2 right	0·33
Hop 1 left & 2 right	0·26	Hop 1 left & 2 right	0·25	Paragraph meaning	0·85
Paragraph meaning	0·85	Paragraph meaning	0·83	Word meaning	0·89
Word meaning	0·85	Word meaning	0·79	Arith. reasoning	0·87
Arith. reasoning	0·87	Arith. reasoning	0·87	Arith. computation	0·83
Arith. computation	0·80	Arith. computation	0·79	Total Stanford Achiev.	0·98
Total Acad. Achiev.	0·89	Total Stanford Achiev.	0·97	Otis IQ	0·90
Otis IQ	0·89	Otis IQ	0·92		

TABLE I—*continued*

Investigators	Total group		Boys		Girls	
Kirkendall (45) 5th and 6th grade children N = 205	Arm coord: 4 counts	0·26	Arm coord: 4 counts	0·26	Hop 2 left & 2 right	0·24
	Arm coord: 6 counts	0·38	Arm coord: 6 counts	0·32	Hop 2 right & 1 left	0·21
	Arm coord: 8 counts	0·39	Arm coord: 8 counts	0·34	Hop 2 left & 1 right	0·23
	Otis IQ	0·91	Otis IQ	0·93	Coord. of arms : 4 counts	0·26
	CFIQ	0·77	CFIQ	0·74	Coord. of arms : 6 counts	0·38
	Paragraph meaning	0·91	Paragraph meaning	0·92	Coord. of arms : 8 counts	0·42
	Word meaning	0·87	Word meaning	0·88	Otis IQ	0·92
	Arith. computation	0·89	Arith. computation	0·91	CFIQ	0·84
	Arith. reasoning	0·82	Arith. reasoning	0·66	Para. meaning	0·90
	Total Achiev.	0·96	Total Achiev.	0·97	Word meaning	0·87
					Arith. computation	0·88
					Arith. reasoning	0·82
					Total Achiev.	0·97
Yoder (71) 4th and 5th grade children N = 340	Hop right & left	0·23	Hop forward right	0·22	Hop 2 left & 2 right	0·24
	Hop left & right	0·23	Hop right & left	0·36	Hop 2 right & 2 left	0·28
	Hop 2 left & 2 right	0·20	Hop forward left	0·21	Word meaning	0·87
	Word meaning	0·84	Hop left & right	0·33	Paragraph meaning	0·89
	Paragraph meaning	0·88	Stand bal. right foot	0·28	Spelling	0·76
	Spelling	0·74	Stand bal. left foot	0·26	Language	0·86
	Language	0·83	Word meaning	0·81	Arith. computation	0·66
	Arith. computation	0·63	Paragraph meaning	0·86	Arith. concepts	0·85
	Arith. concepts	0·83	Spelling	0·75	Social studies	0·79
	Social studies	0·80	Language	0·83	Science	0·79
	Science	0·85	Arith. computation	0·62	Composition	0·80
	Composition	0·80	Arith. concepts	0·84	IQ	0·97
	IQ	0·97	Social studies	0·83		
			Science	0·85		
			Composition	0·80		
			IQ	0·97		

Taken together these few studies would seem to suggest that academic achievement and certain aspects of motor aptitudes are derived from a common source. Certainly the expression of upper and lower limb co-ordination (including balance) seems to depend to a large extent on the same mental source that gives rise to academic achievement among normal children. Some exploration of this possibility has been undertaken by Humphrey (1967) and Ismail (1967). Humphrey has concerned himself with ways of developing academic skills and concepts through motor activity and has suggested active learning situations which appear to be effective. His researches (1962, 1966 and 1967) show that practice sessions combining physical activity and academic concepts induced higher academic achievement scores than traditional methods of presenting mathematics, science and reading materials.

Ismail followed his studies establishing the relationships between motor and intellectual achievements by testing the possible cause and effect reactions. He designed an experiment to determine the effect of an organised course of physical activities on the intellectual performance of fifth and sixth grade children. The experimental group was given three special physical education lessons (in which coordination and balance activities were featured) each week for one school year. A control group, equated for IQ and academic achievement, continued to have their normal physical education classes. At the end of the school year the following results were obtained: (1) there were no significant differences in IQ scores between the experimental and control groups; and (2) there were significant differences in academic achievement in favour of the experimental group to such an extent that they were three to five months more advanced than the control group in reading and arithmetic achievement.

Similar findings have been reported for children with learning difficulties. Oliver's (1958) experiment, for example, with educationally retarded English boys demonstrated that the effects of a systematic programme of physical activities were to be seen not only in improved physical performance but also in academic achievement scores. In the experimental group significant academic gains were recorded, surprisingly, over a relatively short four-week period.

There would seem then to be a good reason to propose that in at least one way the idea of integrated development has strong scientific verification. Motor coordination and intellectual achievement are apparently linked. It appears that among both normal and retarded children the same human resources are being tapped in situations which require the subject to learn and develop coordinated movement as in situations which require the subject to learn to read, write and comprehend. On the face of it this is not surprising since apparently the coordination of movements requires reflective thinking as well as a sensitive sensory motor mechanism and may therefore involve similar cerebral functioning to that needed for other mental performances. If this is so then, in so far as physical education aims to affect not only body but mind also, its programmes must attempt to give maximum stimulus to those neuro-physiological and psychological mechanisms which are accounting for increased intellectual productivity.

Motor aptitudes and personality

A long standing assumption among physical educationists has been that physical abilities (such as those expressed in games and sports) are in some way linked with personality structure. This suggested association between motor performance and personality would, if substantiated, constitute another important dimension of the integrated syndrome which is proposed to explain the interaction of factors accounting for the development and performance of the human organism. Very little rigorous research has been undertaken in this area though Layman (1960) felt able to claim that physical activity and abilities are positively related to mental health, and Scott (1960) in summarising researches up to 1960, concluded that physical abilities are clearly associated with 'desirable' personality characteristics such as confidence, sociability, self-reliance, cooperativeness and personal adjustment. Two recent multivariate analyses have in fact shown that personality may be an important factor in integrated development. In the study by Ismail, Kane and Kirkendall (1969) investigating the relationships between intellectual and non-intellectual (mainly motor aptitudes) variables, eight factors were extracted to account for the variance among pre-adolescent school children. On four of these factors measures of neuroticism and extraversion (Eysenck Personality Inventory) were found to have substantial loadings which was interpreted as indicating a personality link with mental and motor abilities. In a development of his study Kirkendall (1968) confirmed that motor, intellectual and personality (Cattell CPQ) items are significantly interrelated. He also demonstrated that a weighted linear vector of motor coordination measures significantly discriminated between high, medium and low academic achievers. A personality vector similarly discriminated between these three discrete academic groups. No doubt further studies along these lines will continue to clarify the way in which personality fits into the concept of integrated development.

Physical educationists are probably more immediately and vitally interested in the possible relationships between the personality and physical ability domains in so far as the learning and performance of skills may be affected by personality dispositions. While at present it is not too clear how various trait dimensions of personality are linked with the various subdomains of physical ability, there is good reason to suspect that major personality complexes such as Anxiety and Introversion are important dimensions affecting motor performances (see Langer 1966; Whiting and Stembridge 1965). To take this matter further, there are some psychologists (for example Ogilvie and Tutko 1966) who suggest a crucial association between certain personality attributes and high level athletic success. Athletes are proposed in personality terms as a 'special breed' and the suggestion is that, in the last analysis, personality is a vital factor in the discriminating process which singles out the champion from amongst those who seem to have similar physical gifts.

In general then it seems fair to say that the relationship between personality and physical abilities has a widely acknowledged importance in physical education and sports education. One is struck, however, in assessing the present position both by the accepting intuitive reliance placed by many on the existence of this supposed relationship and by the relatively small amount of rigorous research that has been undertaken. It is gratifying, however, to note the increasing number of studies reported in the last five years or so. In many of these the Cattell 16 PF procedures have been used for assessing the personality dimensions and this has had the decided advantage of making possible some comparison between the findings of different investigators. There are nevertheless serious obstacles in the way of the reviewer who wishes to arrive at clear-cut and generalised conclusions from the research evidence now available. Interpretation is made difficult by the variety of systems used for selecting and classifying subjects, by the different analytic methods employed, and most of all by the absence of either well formulated hypotheses or theoretical frameworks.

From the detailed reviews that are available (see Warburton and Kane 1967; Ogilvie 1968 and Husman 1969) it should be possible to postulate a number of testable hypotheses for further rigorous research. These reviews tend to give a personality description of the male athlete or physically gifted person in terms of extravert tendencies (such as high dominance, social aggression, leadership, toughmindedness) and general emotional control reflected in such trait measurements as low anxiety and high confidence. Women with high motor and sporting aptitudes are most often described as being like men athletes on the extraversion dimension, but being unlike them in showing a lower level of emotional control. There are, of course, many exceptions to these general descriptions which have been reported and no doubt both the nature of the physical activity in question and the subject's level of ability and aspiration will in some way be reflected in characteristic ways of behaving. When the activity and level of performance are held constant, interesting consistencies in personality have been reported, and some evidence has even been presented to suggest the existence of certain sports 'types'—for example, a 'soccer type' (Kane 1966), a 'racing driver type' (Ogilvie 1968), and a 'wrestler type' (Kroll 1967). For each of these types a profile (e.g. of the Cattell 16 dimensions) has been proposed which seems to characterise those who are exponents of the particular activity. In the comparison of personality profiles the use of the multivariate discriminant function analysis has become somewhat fashionable. Many earlier studies have relied for interpretation on a simple comparison of the personality measures set out in a profile form. The Cattell 16 PF may, for example, be conveniently set out in profile fashion showing the standardised scores on each of the sixteen dimensions. A number of profiles set out in this way may be compared and the level of agreement between them assessed by a coefficient of profile similarity (r_p). This index is computed by comparing the corresponding profile dimensions one at a time but has the disadvantage that the profile as a whole is never considered, nor is the relative importance of the profile dimensions emphasised. The discriminant function analysis has, by comparison, the special value of taking into account the variability over the entire profile range, so that, in the case of the sixteen personality factors, the total personality is considered when profiles are compared. Only when 'discriminant space' exists between them may profiles be considered to differ.

The special use of this form of analysis in sports personality studies has been particularly well demonstrated by Kroll and Petersen (1965). In this study the investigators compared the 16 PF profiles of five winning and five losing teams. A discriminant function was found which significantly differentiated between winners and losers. The function emphasised the importance of four 16 PF factors in the discriminating process—factor B (general ability), factor H (adventurousness), factor O (confidence) and factor Q3 (willpower). However, a separate univariate analysis between the sixteen profile factors taken one at a time revealed a significant difference for factor B only, thus apparently concealing the importance of other factors which seem to distinguish winners from losers.

Multivariate correlational analyses

It is somewhat surprising to find that there are so few correlational studies which have been undertaken in an attempt to tease out the details of the relationship between the motor and personality domains. If a relationship exists it would seem particularly appropriate to investigate the nature and extent of the association by appropriate correlational procedures so that the particular dimensions accounting for the way in which the two domains are linked might be identified and so that the conditions under which the domains are maximally related might be ascertained. A series of studies using correlational analyses has recently been undertaken (Kane 1968 and 1970) with a view to making a start towards clarifying some of these issues. In these studies the subjects were men and women students who were arranged into four sub-groups according to sex and level of physical (general athletic) ability. Personality was measured by the 16 PF methods and physical performance was assessed by a variety of tests purporting to measure important and well established dimensions of gross physical ability (e.g. static, dynamic and explosive strength, endurance and power), many of which have been identified in the extensive factorial investigations undertaken by Fleishman (1964). Measures of body type (Fat, Muscularity and Linearity) and 'sports participation' were also taken.

Factor structures

From the intercorrelation of the personality and physical measures the factor structures were ascertained for each group of subjects. These factor analyses were completed in order both to identify the major factors accounting for the intercorrelations and to permit a comparison between the factor patterns of the different groups of subjects. For these purposes both primary order and higher order factors were computed in order to provide hypothetical hierarchical structures. Briefly these procedures identified the primary factor structure and then these primary factors were themselves factored in order to produce a more parsimonious second order solution. Further factoring provided the higher orders of the hierarchy which was completed in a final monarchical factor. The network so obtained indicated the way in which factors could be statistically linked at progressively higher levels of analysis.

The solution obtained for the men's groups of subjects (i.e. men of high and moderate physical ability) were remarkably similar and the common hierarchical structure is represented in figure 1 below. Ten first order factors were identified but these gave little or no general indications of the way in which the personality and physical ability measures go together. It is only at the second order of analysis that a clear association emerges—the four factor complexes combining the two domains as follows:

Factor $1'$: Extraversion with general athletic ability.

Factor $2'$: Stability with explosive strength.

Factor $3'$: Toughmindedness with muscularity and sports participation index.

Factor $4'$: Conservatism with endurance.

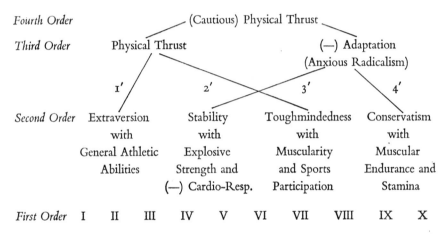

Fourth Order		(Cautious) Physical Thrust		
Third Order	Physical Thrust		(—) Adaptation	
			(Anxious Radicalism)	
	$1'$	$2'$	$3'$	$4'$
Second Order	Extraversion with General Athletic Abilities	Stability with Explosive Strength and (—) Cardio-Resp.	Toughmindedness with Muscularity and Sports Participation	Conservatism with Muscular Endurance and Stamina

| *First Order* | I | II | III | IV | V | VI | VII | VIII | IX | X |

Note: Ten first order factors were extracted. The second order factors were identified and named in terms of their first order loadings.

FIGURE I   *Hierarchical structure—personality with physical abilities*

Previous studies have attempted to argue the personality/physical abilities relationship on the basis of confusing first order correlations between simple unit measures, whereas it would seem from this higher order solution that the relationship has clear meaning only when a number of unit measures are ideally combined as in *extraversion* (which combines five of the 16 PF measures) and in *general athletic ability* (which combines, in this interpretation, measures of speed, strength and power). The multivariate solution appears in this instance to be clearer than the univariate solution. Additionally the second order complexes obtained seem to have high face validity in that major personality dimensions are found in combination with expected physical (athletic) abilities. The third and fourth levels of the factoring are also shown in figure I, but naturally are more difficult to interpret in functional terms. The two third order factors are identified as *Physical Thrust* (with highest loadings on second order factors 1' and 3') and *Anxious Radicalism* (loading on second order factors 2' and 4'—and reflecting perhaps a 'students' temperament'). The final monarchical factor which combines the two third order complexes was found to have highest loadings on extraversion and athletic abilities.

These factorial analyses revealed, therefore, important descriptive information concerning the way in which personality and physical abilities are associated among men. In particular it would seem that the association is to be seen best under circumstances in which the primary units of measure are appropriately combined and weighted. The solution for the women's group did not allow such clear interpretations. Although there were some discernible similarities in the factor structures of the two groups the indications were that real differences may exist in the way in which personality and physical abilities are related among women of superior physical expertise and those of average physical gifts.

Multiple correlation analyses

From the information gained by factor analyses a number of multiple correlation (regression) analyses were computed to investigate further the combination of unit measures that contributed most to the relationship between the two domains. As a result it was found that:

1. Among women Stability (i.e. the combined weighted score on 16 PF traits C, L, O, Q3 and Q4) is significantly associated with the physical abilities vector. Approximately 15 per cent of the variance in Stability is accounted for by the physical ability measures.
2. Among men Extraversion (i.e., 16 PF traits A, E, F, H, Q4) is significantly associated with the physical abilities vector. Approximately 16 per cent of the variance in Extraversion is accounted for by the physical ability measures.
3. The vector of personality variables is significantly associated with an Index of Sports Participation (i.e. degree of sport involvement) among both men and women, accounting for 20 per cent of the variance. The most important personality variables contributing to the correlation were found to be Q2 (Group dependence), E (Dominance) and Q4 (Low ergic tension).

These multiple correlation results expanded the general information obtained from the factor analyses by demonstrating conditions under which the two domains are related. They show in particular that the two main personality complexes, Extraversion and Stability, are moderately but significantly correlated with physical abilities, and moreover that the extent of the subjects' involvement in sporting activities is substantially linked with their degree of extraversion (as represented by 16 PF traits Q2, E and Q4).

The dependent variables chosen for these three analyses were the ones considered most likely to provide most important additional evidence. It was possible, however, that other groupings of the variables might give even clearer evidence of relationships across the two domains. To this end a number of canonical correlation analyses were computed between the sixteen personality predictors and the fifteen physical variables.

Canonical correlation analyses

The canonical correlation is the maximum correlation between the linear functions of two sets of variables and goes a stage further than regression analysis by involving both multiple criteria as well as multiple predictors. The beta weights obtained in canonical analyses indicate the relative contribution which each variable makes to the correlation between the two canonical variates (vectors) and for practical purposes ought to allow a meaningful interpretation. However, the maximising processes involved capitalise on any chance fluctuations or variability occurring in the specific context of a particular sample of cases, so that the beta weights are usually considered to be unstable and apply only in that specific context.

It was somewhat surprising, therefore, that in general the canonical vectors for each sub-group of the subjects gave a somewhat similar picture and appeared to demonstrate high values in athletic ability (i.e., speed, power, endurance) going with Extraversion. All the canonical correlations were significant and ranged from 0·71 for the high motor performance group of men to 0·83 for the equivalent group of women. These consistent and clearly meaningful findings would seem to permit a confident interpretation of a real relationship between total personality and a broad based array of physical abilities. The relationship is particularly supported by those personality traits which combine to form Extraversion and those motor performances which describe general athletic ability.

The general conclusion to be drawn from these correlational studies is that the personality and physical ability domains are clearly associated and that the circumstances under which they are maximally related are best seen when simple unitary measures are appropriately combined in factor complexes.

Summary

Evidence has been presented to support two aspects of the integrated development theory, that between the mental and motor and between personality and motor domains. It would seem that physical education teachers in particular might consider this evidence as being of some importance in helping them to formulate realistic objectives and curricula with particular respect to the non-physical outcomes of their work.

E. A. Peel with the assistance of W. A. de Silva

Some aspects of higher level learning processes during adolescence

The intellectual roots and sap of higher level learning are the ideas respectively required for its progress and formed in it. Indeed we may almost go so far as to identify higher learning with the processes of forming and using concepts through the medium of language and other symbolic systems. The concepts of adolescent learning also depend heavily in their formation and exploitation on context material in which progress is achieved by one-instance learning where the rule is explained and exemplified. The adolescent learner rarely needs an array of instances to lead up to the generalisations required. This need can be by-passed by the use of language. Furthermore this dependence on verbal statements leads to a strengthening of the understanding of the intensive aspect of concepts, that is, their inner nature as expressed in the rules of action and thought governing their existence. This tendency is closely related to the adolescent's growing power—particularly in his later years—to use concepts as abstractions. Thus he is able to use this abstract coinage for carrying out his discussions of institutions, attitudes and theories with a growing confidence as he moves into young adult years.

Finally we may note that much of such discussion calls for judgment, decisions (at least those on paper) and evaluation. This involves the examination of propositions, the terms of which are couched in abstractions. Any examination, therefore, of higher level learning calls for an investigation of the way in which concepts emerge, generalisations and abstractions are formed, and judgments are made through the medium of words and language-thought structures. Precious little has been done, but a few recent studies have been completed and others are in progress which might suggest lines of attack on these interesting problems. I propose to write about three topics which appear to me to be of significance in the development of adolescent thinking:

1. The power to abstract a concept from a contextual setting.
2. The power to form superordinate classes from verbal material.

3.   The relationship between the capacity to use abstract language in the form of writing, and the power to make formal judgments.

The first problem was completed by one of us in the summer of 1969, using material from secondary school history texts (de Silva 1969; Peel 1967). The second is exemplified in a small study on the readiness of the adolescent to form concepts, as opposed to meaningful but alogical connections, when he is presented with *verbal* tests involving the formation of superordinate classes. This really extends the work carried out with non-verbal material—patterns, differently shaped blocks, objects and pictures—on younger children, into the field of the verbal comprehension expected of adolescents. The last topic has been explored in a tentative but suggestive study, carried out by Bartholomew (1970) of the degree of association between the power to make mature judgments and the ability to use abstract language in free writing.

1. Power to abstract a concept

Turning now to the first research, in its most general terms, this was concerned with the problems of one-instance concept learning through the medium of a contextual passage. More specifically, it was concerned also with a longstanding problem faced by history teachers in the intro-duction of new concepts, such as 'entente', 'indulgence' and 'mercantilism'. These names are also quite strange. Often these concepts appear in texts without sufficient explanation and exemplification of them (de Silva 1969; Peel 1967).

Such a problem of identifying concepts tagged only by an unfamiliar name embedded in verbal contexts suggests an application of the technique devised by Werner and Kaplan (1950). They coded words into sentences, each word appearing in six sentences and asked the subjects to give the meaning of the coded word. This sentence method was used by embody-ing each chosen concept word into six different sentences. The same words also occurred each in a single paragraph context, each paragraph being taken from a standard school history text. For both tests ten concept terms were chosen, each being frequently used in history. These were the words: *taxation, monopoly, slump, depression, tariff, capital or money, national-ism, socialism, laissez-faire, cold war, gunboat diplomacy*. The selected school history text containing these words was between 80-100 words long in which the concept word occurred once only. It was then coded by a 'word' unknown to the subjects, e.g. *Slump = Malmir*. The subjects were asked

'What is *Malmir?*' 'Why do you think so?' Here is one of the passages containing the word 'monopoly' coded by *Kohilak*:

K O H I LA K (*Monopoly*)

> *The East India Company was the first and the greatest of the companies which was to play a leading part in the development of the British Empire. Financed chiefly by the City merchants, it held a virtual* K O H I L A K *of trade with India, and was frequently accused of having too restrictive an outlook. Yet for many years it was the only source of capital for English enterprises in India, owned or chartered ships which carried goods to and fro, and made arrangements to market them at their own destination.*

Using a scheme of analysis of the answers based on previous work on the understanding of short textual passages, de Silva (1969) grouped his answers according to categories as follows: logically restricted, circumstantial conceptualisation, logical possibilities, deductive conceptualisation. These categories are as follows:

Logically restricted answers

'These immature responses are not orientated to reality but are tautological, inconsistent, directly contradictory, irrelevant or otherwise irrational and display a gross lack of comprehension of the passage. The subjects responding in this category seem to be put off by irrelevances both of form and content as to deny premises or other conditions of the problem. The responses often take the form of casual irrelevant guesses or bizarre responses. A variety of logically restricted responses was met with.'

Examples of answers were:

KOHILAK

Contract: Because of the way it is linked with the word 'trade'. (Age 13)

Kohilak means past: Because it was in the British Empire. (Age 13)

Kohilak means to ration out things of trade: Because it was accused of having a restrictive outlook. (Age 14)

It means agreement: Because I think it fits the passage. (Age 13)

Small amount. (Age 13)

Circumstantial conceptualisation

'This form of signification is characterised by attempted analysis in terms of one aspect of the presented data and failure to grasp the essential features of the problem. It is an attempt at understanding based on a single piece

E

of circumstantial evidence picked out from the context supporting a simple unqualified inference. Subjects do not show signs of being able to use all the material cues given and are content with very limited, trivial responses. The following examples illustrate this category of responses.'

Answer example:

KOHILAK

Strangle hold: Because it was the only source of capital for English enterprises. They could say what was what and nobody could object. (Age 14)

Logical possibilities

'In this category of response subjects engage in realistic appraisal showing capacity to combine two or more pieces of evidence and ability to relate cause and effect. Possible alternatives and competing solutions are offered and possible explanations invoked. However, they do not stand against all the facts of the situation. The responses made are roughly in harmony with the sense of the passage and are realistically tuned to the problem. . . . This category is the bridge, as it were, between the immature circumstantial conceptualisation on the one hand, and the final, highest step in the development of concept formation through deductive processes on the other.'

Examples of answers were:

KOHILAK

Empire or strong hold: The East India Company felt that if any more freedom was given it might damage their trade if they let any other countries to get a foothold in there, as they feared for their livelihood. (Age 16)

A very high percentage of trade: They were trading a lot. (Age 14)

Dominance: The East India Company was the greatest company and presumably dominated trade with India. (Age 16)

Deductive conceptualisation

'In responses falling within this category the subject generally explores the content of the passage in almost its entirety in a deductive way and draws integrated, reasoned, penetrating and imagined inference taking account essentially of the problem. . . . The primary characteristic of responses in this category is the deductive reasoning or sustained argument from the basis of assumed hypotheses resting on general rules or principles developed inductively or deduced analytically. The correct solution may be viewed as a deductive consequence of an attempt at redescription where according to Danto (1965) the subject has to 'furnish a law, and a law, in fact, which both licenses and is licensed by the redescription'.

Examples of answers were:

KOHILAK

Monopoly: It was a big company and the first to get into India; therefore as it grows, it would make most of the trade of the country. It was about the only one and so it took all the trade or at least most of it. (Age 13)

Monopoly: Because trade by the companies was restricted; this was to stop any competition that could come up and meant that the company was the only company and would charge the prices that it wishes. (Age 14)

Complete control: It states that the East India Company had a restrictive outlook and it was the only source of capital, therefore the East India Company must have had a great grip and very good control of the trading: these facts so say that the East India Company was in complete control of trading. (Age 15)

As already indicated, each concept was also coded into six sentences. Thus *Kohilak* (monopoly) appears as follows:

2.1 A person who has a *kohilak* is in a powerful position.

2.2 A *kohilak* can be very harmful to the people.

2.3 If a manufacturer has a *kohilak* of some article he can charge a very high price.

2.4 It is very difficult to hold a *kohilak* for a long time.

2.5 Other people in order to obtain a share of the profit try to break the *kohilak*.

2.6 The government sometimes prevents the growth of a *kohilak*.

De Silva analysed the answers to the questions 'What is a kohilak?' and 'Why do you think so?' according to a scheme based on that originally used by Werner and Kaplan. There were four categories closely aligned to the categories used by Werner and Kaplan. They are not therefore precisely the same as those chosen for the paragraph test. The four categories—*multi-solution rigidity, single-solution rigidity, progressive construction* and *cumulative conceptualisation*—are explained below.

Multi-solution rigidity

In this level the subject is unable to respond to the requirement that a single code word has only one meaning throughout a given series of sentences. The subject does not carry over indicators from one sentence to another and therefore is unable to accumulate clues that would help a solution. Instead he is satisfied with giving isolated individual responses and ends up with from two to seven different meanings for the identical code word in a single series of six sentences. When invited to offer one overall solution he repeats one of his responses, very often his response to the last, i.e. the sixth sentence. Werner and Kaplan (1950, page 68) witnessed this form of rigidity in their work. 'The child, though recognising that a particular solution fits only one sentence, retains it as the solution for that sentence. The adherence to one solution obstructs attempts to modify or shift to another solution.'

Here is an answer example by a child aged twelve:

2.1 *Gun*: Because you are in a powerful position if you have a gun.

2.2 *Gun*: Because it can be harmful.

2.3 *Lot*: Because if you have a lot you can charge more.

2.4 *Gun*: Because it is difficult to keep a gun without getting caught.

2.5 *Law*: Because they would try to break the law.

2.6 *Drug*: Because the government tries to stop drugs.

Overall solution: drug.

Single-solution rigidity

The subject seizes upon a single piece of evidence either in the opening sentence of the series or in the sentence to which he makes the first response and bases his judgment solely upon this evidence. Subjects are not able to use the material evidence coming in the later sentences of the series and are diverted in their thinking by the apparent importance of the piece of evidence which they chanced to pick up in the beginning. Having thereby arrived at a meaning the subject, leaning on imagined artificial and remote connections, offers this meaning in the case of the other sentences in the series too. This strained ascription of meaning was known to Werner and Kaplan (1950, page 69) as 'forcing a solution'. They say, 'In many instances the child may rigidly adhere to one solution and by forcing the issue may place it, in spite of ill fit, into other sentences. . . . The child will the more succeed in the attempt to force a concept into a sentence the more labile the sentence and word structure is perceived by him.'

Answer example by a child aged thirteen:

2.1 I think the word kohilak is bomb; if you have a bomb you are in a powerful position.

2.2 *Kohilak means bomb*: Because a bomb is very harmful and will kill people.

2.3 *Kohilak means bomb*: Because if a manufacturer is to make the bomb he can charge a high price.

2.4 *Kohilak means bomb*: A bomb is very heavy and might blow up in your face.

2.5 People don't like bombs and will try to break the manufacturer.

2.6 *Kohilak means bomb*: Because a bomb will blow up a country and kill thousands of people.

Overall solution: bomb.

Progressive construction

Realistic appraisal showing capacity to combine more than one piece of evidence and ability to accumulate relevant cues from sentence is seen as a competing solution, generally at a different level of abstraction than the correct solution and lacking in precision and exactitude. All attempts at solution which finally end up with a possible alternative, regardless of the number of steps gone through, fall within this category. The following instances illustrate this category of response, by a child aged fourteen:

2.1 *No response.*

2.2 *Bomb*: Because that a bomb can be very dangerous to many people's lives.

2.3 *Right*: Because it is up to the manufacturer to name his price for the goods.

2.4 *Right*: Because other people can always copy your idea.

2.5 *Right*: Because like anything today it is found out by someone else so that they cannot hold the right.

2.6 *Right or patent*: Because the government probably only have the patents out for such a time like a couple of years.

Overall solution: right or patent.

Cumulative conceptualisation

In this category of response the subject progressing from sentence to sentence confirms, modifies or replaces a preliminary solution until he arrives at the final concept. As the subject progresses from sentence to sentence he is actively aware of the gathering cumulative evidence, profiting from which he eliminates alternatives and ends up by offering the correct solution or an acceptable form of it in other words or phrases. Subjects making responses falling in this category show indications that they have blasted the 'concrete barrier' and have developed what Werner and Kaplan (1950, page 63) term an 'abstract-symbolic attitude' and are able to view the sentence content 'as an ideal, timeless event lifted out of the sphere of actuality and placed into the sphere of possibility'.

It does not always happen that the subject is able to offer the correct solution in response to the first sentence. Often it is later in the series that he is able to offer the correct solution. All attempts at solution which finally end up with the correct solution, regardless of the number of steps, fall within this category.

Answer example by a child aged fourteen:

2.1   *Seat in Parliament*: They can try to enforce new laws and control areas of the country.

2.2   *An army*: An army can be used for killing and destroying crops, etc.

2.3   *Monopoly*: If someone has the only obtainable supply of something important to the people a high price can be charged because he has no competition.

2.4   *Monopoly*: Others of the same thing will be obtained and the prices brought down through competition.

2.5   *Monopoly*: People who want to get into the market of the goods must first break the stranglehold that the person or company has over its distribution, etc.

2.6   *Monopoly*: If one grows it can be difficult to break and cause difficulties to the people.

Overall solution: a monopoly of certain goods or objects which makes the prices very high because there can be no competition from other competitors.

The main differences shown between different age groups and between the grammar and non-grammar type of pupil are brought out in the following tables. The first pair of tables refers to the Passages Test.

TABLE I   *Frequency of responses to the passages test categorised by age group for the whole of the population*

	Age and number in sample				
Answer categories	12 yrs 20	13 yrs 40	14 yrs 40	15 yrs 40	16 yrs 20
No response	8	14	26	38	11
Limited response	142	275	252	189	80
Circumstantial conceptualisation	20	37	42	62	33
Logical possibility	9	24	17	35	7
Deductive conceptualisation	21	50	63	76	69
Total number of responses	200	400	400	400	200

The trend by age is brought out more clearly by converting the above frequencies to percentages of the total for each age group.

TABLE 2   *Percentages of frequency*

Response category	Age				
	12 yrs	13 yrs	14 yrs	15 yrs	16 yrs
No response	4·0	3·5	6·5	9·5	5·5
Limited response	71·0	68·8	63·0	47·0	40·0
Circumstantial conceptualisation	10·0	9·3	10·5	15·5	16·5
Logical possibility	4·5	6·0	4·3	8·8	3·5
Deductive conceptualisation	10·5	12·5	15·8	19·0	34·5

Turning to the Sentences Tests, we have the following corresponding results:

TABLE 3   *Number of responses in each category by age group— sentences test*

Response category	Age and number in sample				
	12 yrs 20	13 yrs 40	14 yrs 40	15 yrs 40	16 yrs 20
No response	8	12	8	5	1
Multi-solution rigidity	133	272	198	165	66
Single-solution rigidity	27	53	86	82	40
Progressive construction	14	32	47	65	21
Cumulative conceptualisation	18	31	61	83	72
Total number of responses	200	400	400	400	200

TABLE 4   *Percentages of responses in each category by age group— sentences test*

Response category	Age and number in sample				
	12 yrs 20	13 yrs 40	14 yrs 40	15 yrs 40	16 yrs 20
	%	%	%	%	%
No response	4·0	3·0	2·0	0·1	0·5
Multi-solution rigidity	66·5	68·0	49·5	41·3	33·0
Single-solution rigidity	13·5	13·3	21·5	20·5	20·0
Progressive construction	7·0	8·0	11·8	16·3	10·5
Cumulative conceptualisation	9·0	7·8	15·3	27·5	36·0

The above tables show quite a marked moving towards more mature concept formation at ages fifteen to sixteen years, and these trends at these ages were found to be statistically significant.

When we come to compare grammar and non-grammar groups we have the following overall frequency of responses with regard to each of the tests.

TABLE 5   *Comparison of the grammar and non-grammar groups—passages test*

Group	NR	LR	CC	LP	DC
Non-grammar	62	544	76	30	88
Grammar	35	394	118	62	191

NR = No response
LR = Logically restricted
CC = Circumstantial conceptualisation
LP = Logical possibilities
DC = Deductive conceptualisation

TABLE 6   *Comparison of the grammar and non-grammar groups—sentences test*

	NR	MSR	SSR	PC	CC
Non-grammar	17	448	165	80	90
Grammar	17	386	123	99	175

NR = No response
MSR = Multi-solution rigidity
SSR = Single-solution rigidity
PC = Progressive construction
CC = Cumulative conceptualisation

Again the difference between the two groups is statistically significant. This was confirmed also by scoring the responses on a 0–4 basis, giving no responses '0' and the most mature responses '4'. When de Silva considered the growth of mature concept formation by age for each group separately, he obtained results as illustrated in the following graph. The ages fifteen to sixteen seemed to make the significant appearance of concept formation at the most mature level.

It will be seen that mature concept formation from contextual material is only achieved at the earliest by the age of fifteen. This confirms results obtained from a related investigation by Rhys (1966) on the development of logical thinking in secondary school geography and by Stones (1967) on the comprehension of history by secondary school pupils, and the investigation by Hallam (1966) of the maturity of moral-historical judgments of adolescents. Although none of these three studies is concerned specifically with concept formation, the process enters by implication into their problem tasks.

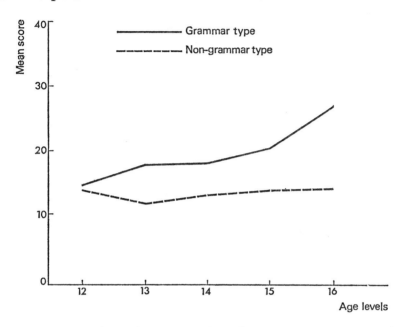

From de Silva's results it seems that whatever new ideas, institutions and names of new Acts are introduced into school historical discussions, they should be supported by more than the contextual prose in which they first appear. Examples should be cited and the functioning and conditions of existence of any such institutions should also be discussed.

2. Classification and concept formation

We may also easily demonstrate that adolescents have some difficulties, which we normally associate with childhood, in the act of classifying, particularly if the material is verbal. If for instance they are asked to identify superordinate classes by their names among lists of terms which include partially associated entities and meaningful, contiguous and similar but illogically connected elements, the majority are not likely in early adolescence to form inclusive classes. In circumstances calling for the use of understanding of words, even by fifteen years of age a sizeable minority seem still not able to recognise the inclusions

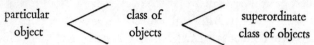

particular object < class of objects < superordinate class of objects

Here are the results of an investigation carried out with two groups of adolescents of average ability and of mean ages 12+ and 16+, compared with a group of adults of superior ability. The test situation was as follows:

This is a test of your understanding of words and phrases. Each test consists of two rows of words or phrases. In the first row there are three words or phrases which are related to each other in a certain way. You are to discover this relationship and then to use it as a guide for completing the second row. This you do by underlining what you think is the correct word or phrase wherever there is a column of five alternatives.

Here is an example which is done for you:

Robin Hood	outlaw	man
daisy	flower	horticulture
		petal
		bush
		<u>plant</u>
		bouquet

Now do these two by first examining the three parts of the first row to find how they are related and then picking the word or phrase in the column of the second row which most nearly completes the same relationship as in the first row.

1. Ford	car	vehicle
Harrogate	town	Yorkshire
		city
		population centre
		local government
		health resort
2. Westminster Abbey	church	building
Bobby Charlton	footballer	Manchester United player
		English International
		baldheaded man
		sportsman
		brother of Jackie Charlton

The results are given in the following table where the correct response, the superordinate class name, has been underlined. The percentages of generalisation responses and other responses are given in the last rows against each test item.

TABLE 7   *Frequency of responses*

	1st year 12+	5th year 16+	Adults
Yorkshire	11	7	2
city	13	10	—
population centre	6	9	28
local government	1	2	—
health resort	1	2	2
% Generalisation responses	18·7	30·0	77·5
% Other responses	81·3	70·0	12·5
Manchester United player	11	4	1
English International	1	4	—
baldheaded man	—	—	—
sportsman	15	22	31
brother of Jackie Charlton	4	—	—
% Generalisation responses	48·4	73·3	96·9
% Other responses	51·6	26·7	3·1

The variously partial, contiguous, associated but logically irrelevant answers are seen against the four alternatives in the multiple choice. At least Bobby Charlton's bald head is seen as an irrelevance!

A later investigation included the following item:

Queen Elizabeth II   ship   passenger carrier

Henry VIII   king   Tudor
                                   Royal person
                                   Anne Boleyn
                                   Prince
                                   Kind of ruler

with the results as shown:

Response	Adults	5th year	3rd year	1st year
n	94	70	66	63
1. Tudor	5	8	16	12
2. Royal person	32	39	37	45
3. Anne Boleyn	—	—	—	1
4. Prince	—	—	—	1
5. Kind of ruler	57	23	13	4

Percentage responses				
1. Tudor	5·3	11·4	24·2	19·0
2. Royal person	34·0	55·7	56·1	71·4
3. Anne Boleyn	—	—	—	1·6
4. Prince	—	—	—	1·6
5. Kind of ruler	60·6	32·8	19·7	6·4
	94·6	88·5	75·8	77·8

This item shows the intrusion of a linguistic ambiguity caused by the term 'kind of ruler'. Henry VIII is a kind of ruler, that is, he is a class to himself only by virtue, say, of having had six wives. As a kind of ruler he is unique and strictly speaking this response is an abstraction (Peel 1971).

It would appear that in popular language usage 'kind of ruler' is used as being equivalent to ruler, and that this tendency becomes more marked as a person gets older. It would therefore be more revealing if we summed responses to numbers 2 and 5 to see how far the individuals formed a logical superordinate class. When this is done, we obtained the percentages as shown in the bottom line of the above table. There is, even with the complication mentioned, a stronger tendency in younger children to give the alogical responses to: Tudor, Anne Boleyn, Prince.

Concept formation has its roots in the logical similarities and differences between the members of any array of material. But what the immature thinker sees as similarities may not be logically based. Also in the above 3-step situation the wrong response gives evidence of a shift of criteria by which to judge similarity. This is a feature frequently noted in research on concept formation (Werner and Kaplan 1950; Bruner, Olver and Greenfield 1966; de Silva 1969).

3. *The relationship between the capacity to write abstractly and judge formally*

Bartholomew* measured the level of maturity of adolescents' judgments by giving them eight problems of a contemporary topical and political kind. These included the two following:

E. Older people think decimal coinage is hard to understand and they do not like the idea of a metric system of measurement. Last month a baby died because a hospital nurse made a mistake with the new decimal measure and gave him too much of a drug.
    Should we change to the decimal system?
    Why do you think this?

F. These days people live longer than they used to because medical care is better. Older people feel the cold more than younger ones and they like to have a blazing coal fire. Because of smoke and fog in winter the Government has decided that some districts shall be smokeless zones and people there will not be allowed to burn coal on their fires any more.
    Is the Government right?
    Why do you think this?

She also asked each subject to write on a single topic 'Home' and the first hundred words of each pupil's composition were analysed according to the method of Flesch (1950) for definiteness of writing and ideas. The Flesch formula includes the counting of finite verbs, nouns with a natural gender and their modifying adjectives, the definite article and its noun, and other words having a definite specific direction. The results of the Flesch method of counting may be illustrated from two extreme passages used by him to demonstrate the method in his original paper. They are as follows:

> '*The children were telling* about *their Christmas vacations.*
> '*We went* to Kansas,' *said Jack.* '*One day when we were skating* on *the lake* some of the *boys cut* a hole in *the ice, struck* a match and a fire *blazed* right up out of *the hole* for *two* or *three minutes.*'
> '*Oh, oh!' said* all the others, '*that* couldn't be true, water *doesn't* burn.'
> '*But it is* true,' *said Jack.* '*I saw it.*'
> *They turned* to *the teacher* to see *what she would* say and *she explained this* very strange *happening. It seems* there are natural gas wells under *the* lake . . .
>
> 54 definite words in 100
> Highly concrete.

* Reported with the kind permission of Mrs M. Bartholomew.

'Truth is thought which *conforms* to the form of the whole. Conformity to the whole is *the criterion*. The unitary truth is *that* which *conforms* to the whole process of which *it* is a part. *The truth* is a form embedded in the whole complex of processes in the human organism and *its environment*, symbolising and organising *them*. A particular truth *may* not represent the entire structure of a situation but only *those aspects* which are relevant at a given stage in *its development*. *The truth* is a system of symbols *whose structure conforms* to the whole pattern.'

21 definite words in 100 Abstract.

Bartholomew divided her population of pupils into two groups, first-year and fourth-year children at a non-selective secondary school. First she compared the total judgment score obtained by scoring answers to the judgment problems between the whole group of pupils (first-years and fourth-years) she tested and the group whose writing was analysed by the Flesch method. The mean judgment scores for these two groups were *30·8* and *31·3* respectively.

Then she compared the judgment scores for the twenty first-year and twenty fourth-year pupils taking the Flesch test. The mean judgment scores were respectively *27·24* and *34·36* ($t = 6·28$, $p < 0·01$). We see that, as we would expect, there is a significant difference between the maturity of judgments exercised by the first and fourth-year groups.

In the following comparisons of mean Flesch scores we must remind ourselves that a high measure means a high degree of definiteness, and a low degree of abstractness. Different groups had mean Flesch scores as follows:

First-year	35·55
Fourth-year	33·0
F = 0·76 (not significant)	
Boys	33·8
Girls	34·75
F = 0·10 (not significant)	
20 poorest judgers	38·50
20 best judgers	30·05
F = 10·38 ($p < 0·01$)	

The similarity between boys' and girls' groups is not surprising but one might have expected a significant difference between the definiteness of the writing of the first-year and fourth-year groups. However, as is seen, this difference, although in the right direction, turned out not to be significant. What is most interesting is that the twenty best judgers, as compared with the twenty poorest judgers were significantly more capable of writing more abstractly.

When she made the complementary comparison between the mean judgment scores of the twenty pupils with the highest Flesch counts and the twenty with the lowest Flesch count, she obtained the following mean judgment scores:

20 highest Flesch scorers   28·5
20 lowest Flesch scorers   34·1
$F = 6·11 \ (p < 0·05)$

Here again we have an expected difference appearing at a statistically significant level.

This work, although only tentative and exploratory, nonetheless has given promising results and needs to be followed up by using more recent methods for assessing the abstractness of the children's writing, as suggested by Gillie (1957) and by adding other tests of their readiness to recognise abstract notions as devised by Peel (1971) and introduced elsewhere.

In all three areas studied, we have demonstrated features of intellectual development during adolescence which appear to be significant in relation to the thinking required and assumed through the medium of language, in the middle and upper classes of secondary schools. These include one-instance learning of concepts from verbal contexts, the capacity to form logical superordinate classes from class names, and the relation between maturity of judgment in verbal situations and the power to write abstractly.

Sheila M. Chown

Intelligence in adulthood and old age

The years of childhood are years of growth and development. The intellectual changes which occur lead to greater powers of abstraction and greater problem-solving ability. During childhood and adolescence, the individual, whether he likes it or not, has new and varied experiences constantly thrust upon him. His social life, too, alters as its centre moves from the family, to the peer-group and back to the family but now of his own choosing. The focus of his intellectual life normally moves from home to school to work. The adult, with his occupation fixed and his family established, experiences in the normal way fewer drastic environmental changes than the child. Most adults want to keep their work and family situations stable, whereas the child is being taught to expect change. In Erikson's terms, the first four crises of life are concerned with learning trust, self-control, sexual identity and habits of work, while those of adolescence and later are concerned with achieving ego-identity, intimacy with others, nurturing the next generation and making sense of one's own life pattern (Lidz 1970). Put crudely, the problems of the adult are those of maintaining and making sense of behaviour patterns already established, and of coping with losses which disturb those patterns. This reflects the adult's position also with respect to logical reasoning and powers of abstract thinking.

The study of changes in intelligence in the normal, ageing, adult is so often a study of 'changes for the worse' that it can be a depressing business. However, the ultimate aims of such research are positive. First, there is the hope that, once normal age changes have been delineated, work can proceed on ways to ameliorate the changes. For example, the effectiveness of various teaching methods for people of different ages can be explored (Belbin 1958). Second, there is the chance of cooperation with physiologists and biochemists, searching for means to slow down if not reverse the biological changes with age. Such people require test materials with which to measure the mental effects (if any) of their treatments. However, it is no simple matter to study the effects of ageing, because it is only too true that 'age does not come alone'.

Can we study pure ageing?

There are people who believe that age changes are in fact all due to the results of health changes. The older the adult, the more likely he is to suffer from high blood pressure, bronchial troubles, and deafness, to name but three common chronic ailments. Some health troubles appear to affect performance on intelligence tests. For instance, arteriosclerosis and high blood pressure appear to be accompanied by lower intelligence test scores (Birren and Spieth 1962; Spieth 1964). Deafness (Farrimond 1961) and poor vision (Weale 1965) may also affect test scores since such sensory deficiencies interfere with the perception of test material and with grasp of instructions. (Incidental effects are also likely since chronic ailments often alter the frequency or quality of social interaction, and may well lead to depression and loss of morale.) People interested in the psychological effects of age must be interested in the effects of these concomitants of age. However, it is not good enough to view these effects as the primary results of chronological age. They are the results of illnesses which can occur (though less frequently) in younger as well as older adults. When they do, they are followed by similar effects. Quite subtle differences in health can affect test scores. Birren *et al.* (1963) studied a group of elderly men who passed a stringent medical and physiological examination, and showed that their intellectual performance on verbal and performance tests was better than that of a group of men who did not pass the medical quite so well.

However, even in an extremely healthy group there are still age differences in intelligence. Birren and Spieth (1962) carried out a programme of testing using 156 civil airline pilots between the ages of twenty and sixty as their subjects. These men had all just passed a strict medical examination, designed to weed out those unfit to continue as airline pilots. Birren and Spieth nevertheless found that the older pilots were less quick at reaction time tasks, at a digit-symbol substitution task and at form perception tasks. This study makes clear that when we look at age differences in performance we are not looking merely at changes due to gross defects in health or sensory equipment. But, in fact, few pieces of research have controlled for state of health to the extent that Birren did. Most have been content to take as subjects any people well enough to come to a central office to be tested. We can therefore expect that the results from most studies will exaggerate somewhat the deleterious effects of 'pure age'.

The cross-sectional approach

If groups of people from similar backgrounds who are currently aged twenty, thirty, forty, fifty, sixty and seventy are tested on Raven's *Progressive Matrices* (Raven 1938b), the scores will show a steady linear decline from young to old. Such results have been obtained by Foulds and Raven (1948) using an army population, and by Heron and Chown (1967) using a volunteer sample from one industrial area of England. Taken at face value, it looks as though intelligence of the kind measured by the *Matrices* does decline steadily with age.

Yet if the same sets of people are tested on information items or vocabulary tasks, there will be no fall off in score between age groups. The distinction appears to be that between *reasoning afresh* (coping with new logical problems) and *producing stored information* (giving a ready-made answer to a familiar question). Few tasks demand nothing but pure reason; few require nothing but stored information. So, in a test like the Wechsler Adult Intelligence Scale (Wechsler 1944 and Wechsler 1958a) the sub-tasks will vary considerably in the extent to which they appear to cause 'fall-off' in performance with age. In 1958, Wechsler listed the tests (Wechsler 1958b) which show little differentiation between age groups as (going from least to most alteration) Information, Vocabulary, Comprehension, Arithmetic, Similarities and Digit Span. Those tests which show a good deal of decrement with age are (again from least to most) Picture Completion, Object Assembly, Block Design, Picture Arrangement and Digit Symbol. These two groups fall into the two broad categories of tasks requiring verbal skills and those requiring performance responses. However, as the verbal tasks all call upon ready-made answers (or at worst, overlearned skills such as arithmetic) while the performance tasks all require the application of reasoning or new learning, it seems more rewarding to dichotomise the tasks according to the degree of reasoning required to carry them out. The tasks which show little alteration across age groups have been christened 'hold' tests, and those which do alter have been called 'don't hold' tests. These terms, rather than 'verbal' and 'performance' will be used in this paper.

In order to cope with the age differences in results, Wechsler introduced the idea of age-related norms, whereby raw score on any sub-test was measured against raw scores obtained by other people of the same age as the individual now being considered. The relative standing of the person within his own age groups could thus be ascertained, and a verdict given in terms of his *age adjusted* intelligence quotient. It is usual to quote a verbal and performance IQ—both age adjusted—when dealing with clinical cases. However, for research on ageing itself it is more usual to be concerned with raw scores and raw age-decrements.

Establishing norms entailed testing many people from each age group. This revealed an interesting fact, that the older the group being tested, the greater the spread or range of raw scores recorded. The raw score norms for Raven's *Matrices* (Foulds and Raven 1948) illustrate this fact. Lines joining the medians of the upper third of scorers, the middle third of scorers and the lower third of scorers at each age gradually get further apart as we go from young to old. Two hypotheses can be suggested which could account for such findings. The first is that age may have a differential effect upon the initially bright and the initially dim. In this case, differences in scores achieved by those of different ages would be greater among the dim and smaller among the bright. In order to examine this hypothesis properly, we would need to follow up the same people during their adult lives, re-testing them many times. Only in this way would we know who did start out bright and who dim. However, we can choose to make the assumption (since vocabulary does not, in a 'normal' population, fall off with age) that a person's vocabulary score *now* will give us a measure strongly related to his reasoning power when he was young. (At age twenty, Raven's *Matrices* and *Mill Hill Vocabulary* (Raven 1938a) scores correlate approximately 0·6—far from perfect, but nevertheless high.) Having made the assumption, we can match people of different ages for their present vocabulary scores, and then compare their scores on the *Matrices* test. The data in table 1 were obtained from a sample of 540 men and women from the north-west of England (Heron and Chown 1967). It looks as though those old people with high vocabulary scores show less difference from young ones in their *Matrices* scores than do old people with low vocabulary scores. It is of some interest to note that the differential age difference is only apparent in the oldest age groups. Thus, while it looks as though the first hypothesis may be correct, we may have here a health effect rather than an age effect.

The second hypothesis is that 'use' of intellect may have a beneficial effect upon the maintenance of intelligence. (This is quite compatible with the first hypothesis.) To examine this we can take people who score within a narrow band on the vocabulary scale, and thus who can be assumed to be matched for 'initial ability'. We can look at the *Matrices* scores for those in non-manual jobs (Registrar General's classes I and II) and compare them with the *Matrices* scores for those in manual jobs (Registrar General's classes IV and V). From the data in table 2, again based on the sample from the north-west of England, but now only of 88 cases, it appears that there is less difference between those old and young adults in non-manual jobs than in manual jobs. Again, however, differences only become large in the oldest groups, and so again it may be that we have a health rather than an age effect.

Research on psychological aspects of ageing, including age differences in intellectual functioning, has usually been cross-sectional. It has tested *different* people at various ages, and in comparing results across age groups has suggested that differences found are due to the effects of age. The

TABLE I   Matrices *scores in age groups matched for* Mill Hill Vocabulary

Vocabulary	Age			Age differences	
	30	50	70	50–30	70–30
High	53	49	41	4	12
Medium	49	45	31	4	18
Low	44	38	21	6	23

TABLE 2   Matrices *scores in age groups for type of work: all subjects had medium vocabulary scores*

Type of work	Age			Age differences	
	30	50	70	50–30	70–30
Registrar General I & II	51	46	37	5	14
Registrar General IV & V	46·5	42	26	4·5	20·5

cross-sectional approach has been favoured due to financial expediency, since it means that results can be obtained more quickly and more cheaply than when individuals have to be followed up over time.

However, it assumes that the people in the various age groups are sufficiently similar for differences in performance to be due to age effects. Even if the groups are similar in most respects, there will be cultural differences between them due to changes in the educational and social climate. People now aged sixty were taught to accept the statements of their teachers without question, and were expected to learn by rote. Tests and test procedure were not part of the accepted routine of their schooldays. They had fewer contacts (albeit vicarious) with the wider world through the mass media. These are examples of differences in cultural experience which favour younger adults. Differences in scores between age groups might be partly due to such extraneous factors of culture rather than to age itself.

Longitudinal studies

Because of objections such as these, longitudinal follow-up studies of people as they age would seem to be needed to provide more accurate results. However, even in longitudinal work there are difficulties. The effects of practice on tests and of increase in test sophistication have to be taken into account. There have been difficulties in selecting tests which will cover a sufficient range of abilities to make the long-term study seem worth while. Keeping in touch with subjects is not easy (nor is it cheap). There is the suspicion that studying the person may in itself have some effect upon the social and environmental (if not psychological) effects of ageing. There is the problem of drop-outs—subjects with whom contact is lost. Inevitably some people do disappear from a study, through geographical mobility, or disinclination to continue to help or illness or death. Dropping out has proved to be selective rather than random, and therefore is an important matter for longitudinal research. Lastly, from the point of view of research workers, money and assistants willing to back up a study already planned and begun but not likely to produce results for some years are not easy to find and these mundane facts make longitudinal work unattractive to undertake.

There have been one or two instances of long-term studies which have happened due to lucky finds of old test material. Owens (1959), for example, was able to trace 201 out of 363 Iowa students who had first been tested in 1919. He obtained the cooperation of 127 of these to retake the test, the *Army Alpha*, in 1949. In an article entitled 'Is age kinder to the initially more able?' Owens explained that no systematic age declines appeared to have occurred during the thirty years interval, during which his subjects had matured from an average age of nineteen to forty-nine. In fact, on four of the sub-tests, some improvement appeared to have occurred (though this was unrelated to initial ability).

It is necessary to be cautious about these results, for two reasons. First, Owens' subjects were originally a somewhat superior group compared with the population as a whole. And those who agreed to be re-tested were themselves a superior sample of those originally tested. Such people might indeed be expected to show rather little fall off by age fifty, especially since most would be in non-manual occupations. An even more serious objection is that the *Army Alpha* test is itself a verbal (and numerical) test, which, if we had to classify it in terms of Wechsler's 'hold' and 'don't hold' categories, would come within the bounds of the 'hold' tests. For this reason, too, the overall fall off on such test material would be expected to be small.

In 1961 Owens re-tested for a second time 97 out of his first re-test group of 127 (Owens 1966). On this occasion, for the group, by then aged about sixty-one, he found that there was some fall off, on the least verbal items (i.e. on the numerical items). The differences in overall scores were not significantly great—but then we would not expect them to be so even on numerical items.

Another 'accidental' study was carried through by Nisbet (1957) in Aberdeen. He found a batch of test records of students who completed their postgraduate teacher-training year in 1930, when their average age was twenty-three. He was able to trace and re-test 141 of them in 1955 (aged forty-seven), and carried out a further re-test of 80 of these in 1964 (aged fifty-six). The test they had been given was the Simplex, again a test which consists of verbal and numerical items and which would have to be classified by us as a 'hold' test. Nisbet found that at first re-test the scores on all sub-tests had actually increased to a significant extent. At the second re-test, (Nisbet and Burns 1965) performance had declined sharply on the numerical sub-tests causing an overall drop in total score compared with the scores at the second testing. Nisbet's group was again a highly selected one, and intriguing too in that it consisted of people engaged in teaching or allied professions. Perhaps the most interesting finding is that by the age of fifty-six any decline at all should have been apparent in such a group on the numerical items.

The most famous longitudinal study of intelligence was planned, but not as a study of adults. Terman's 'gifted children' are now middle aged, and Bayley and Oden (1955) devised a special test, the concept mastery test, to provide a test difficult enough for the high-level sample. The test has been given twice to the sample, once in 1940 and once in 1952. The results show that the subjects have high powers of abstraction, and that these powers have, if anything, increased during those twelve years. Unfortunately, when the test was devised, Wechsler's work was not published, and so again we are faced with a test which relies heavily upon verbal skill (though reasoning is also involved).

There have been one or two planned longitudinal studies carried out with ordinary healthy people as subjects, which have concentrated on those aged fifty or more at the beginning of the study, and which have used tests which come from the 'don't hold' as well as the 'hold' repertoire. Jarvik *et al.* (1962) started out with 268 people over sixty-five, literate and living at home. They followed them up for eight years, re-testing them after one year and again after a further seven years. In all 79 people re-took the tests three times. When the results from the second re-test were compared with their initial scores, performance was lower on the digit symbol and block design from the Wechsler Adult Intelligence Scale (WAIS) both of which are 'don't hold' tests. Speed of tapping as fast as possible was also lower. On the other hand, there were no declines on similarities, digit span (both 'hold' tests) and on a vocabulary test. Jarvik and her colleagues found that their original subjects were above the average for their age at the initial testing, and that those who were still there at the second re-testing were above the average for the original sample. In other words, self-selection appeared to have taken place among the subjects so that for one reason or another the sample finally reported upon was of well above average ability.

Another study which comprised a representative sample in the first instance was that by Riegel and colleagues (Riegel and Riegel 1962; Riegel *et al.* 1963; Riegel 1966). The main purpose of their work was to standardise a German version of the WAIS, and they tested a sample of people of various ages living in Hamburg. Five years later, 202 of the 308 people aged fifty-five or above were re-tested. Comparison of the re-test data with the original scores showed that those just over the age of fifty-five had improved, but that the older ones had shown a decline on those performance sub-tests which occur in the 'don't hold' list of WAIS sub-tests. The declines were slightly less than the age differences in Riegel's original cross-sectional scores for those subjects. Again, a comparison of the initial scores of those re-tested with those who had died showed that death had taken a selective toll, more often occurring among the initially less able. Those who had lost contact with the research for other reasons also proved to be, on average, initially less able than those recontacted. These results, with subjects well enough to live at home and come and be tested when invited, suggest that cross-sectional findings do not exaggerate the effects of age very much, and that declines in reasoning ability do occur in late middle age.

Other investigators have studied special groups of ageing adults, living in institutions. For example, Berkowitz and Green (1963) tested 184 men living in Veteran's Administration hospitals. Their average age was fifty-six at that time, and they were re-tested after an interval of between five and fourteen years. Their average performance on *all* the sub-tests of the WAIS, 'hold' as well as 'don't hold', went down in that time, and on all sub-tests by about the same amount.

A rather different age of sample, but also an institutionalised one, was studied by Kleemeier (1962) at Moosehaven, Florida. He began by testing 70 men, aged sixty-five and over, and followed them up until death or until, twelve years later, he had given three re-tests. He ended with thirteen men. He found that performance was up at the first re-test, but thereafter declined, and declined on all sub-tests of the WAIS.

A distinction must therefore be drawn between people living in the community and people who have had recourse to life within an institution. 'Hold' tests may not always hold up with age if the population being tested is not representative of the normal free-living population. The reasons for this may well vary. Lack of stimulation may be the most plausible explanation in the case of the Veteran's Administration sample. While this may apply to the Moosehaven group also, the onset of patho-logical changes seems a possibility which should not be ignored in that case.

Kleemeier (1962) noticed that many of the men in his sample showed a somewhat large drop in intelligence test score six months to two years before death. The unexpectedly large drop was only found in the records of *some* of those who died, but was never found in the records of those who survived longer than two years after being tested. Moreover, there appeared to be no relation between the cause of death (accident, short term illness, long term illness) and the existence or not of the discrepant drop in score. Kleemeier found that the drop *was* related to vague complaints by the subjects themselves that 'the world seemed different'. He believed that the drop reflected a change in the physio-logical state of the individual rather than a normal change with age. While the nature of the physiological change has yet to be deter-mined, it seems likely that Kleemeier was seeing here the onset of patho-logical age changes as compared to the normal age changes which had gone on before.

Senile performance

In normal ageing, the person displays some lack in ability, yet is able to carry on life in the outside world (provided his physical health permits). There is much argument still as to whether the disorientations of thinking and memory which are symptoms of the senile dementias are themselves different only in quantity or also in quality from the changes seen in normal ageing. Much may turn on this argument, since what is being suggested is that the organic changes which underly the senile dementias could be thought of as occurring in lesser degrees in normal ageing and so accounting for age changes. It does seem to be the case that senile old people do even less well than normal old people on a number of 'don't hold' tests—but not necessarily on all of them. Botwinick and Birren (1951) reported poorer performance by a senile group on the object assembly sub-test only, for example, while Orme (1957) found poorer performance by a senile group on Raven's *Matrices*.

However, there do seem to be qualitative differences in both memory and reasoning ability between the normal aged and the senile person. Though memory defects occur in the normal aged person, they tend to be for loss of details rather than of major events, and to be for happenings in the past rather than for the present or previous few hours. Kral (1962) has pointed out that senile memory fails for major events and the immediate present and past. Similarly, the normal aged person can learn new vocabulary or word associations, whereas the senile person cannot (Kendrick *et al.* 1965).

When we look at 'hold' tests, the performance of the senile is often found to be disturbed when compared with that of normal people of the same age. Botwinick and Birren (1951) found that the information sub-test and the vocabulary sub-test of the WAIS were poor in their senile group. Orme (1957) found that a senile group were worse than a normal aged group on the *Mill Hill Vocabulary* test. Thus, vocabulary and information measures cannot be used with senile persons to give an assessment of pre-illness level of performance. There is evidence that rather similar changes in performance on vocabulary accompany diffuse brain damage in young persons (Davies 1968), although vocabulary holds up on normal ageing.

The evidence (Corsellis and Evans 1963) suggests that senile performance appears when there are marked arteriosclerotic changes, or gross cortical changes and deteriorations. But it is harder to pinpoint the physiological accompaniments of intellectual changes due to normal ageing. Obrist *et al.* (1963) found no relation between EEG records and test results in normal adults, though there was a relation in the very deteriorated. Birren *et al.* (1963) found no relation between oxygen uptake by the brain and test performance in very healthy adults, although there is such a relation in the senile. Nevertheless, there *is* a constant decline in the number of live cortical cells, and there *are* general declines in the functional capacity of living cells as they age. At the moment, it seems most sensible to regard senile age changes as different from these physiological changes of normal ageing.

Loss of speed

Cross-sectional studies probably give too harsh a picture of age deficits on two counts. First, they ignore the cultural factors which act against the older subjects. Second, the older age groups may contain more people who have experienced the 'sharp drop' in intelligence reported by Kleemeier and who should not really be in a 'normal' group. On the other hand, such studies may give too liberal a view of the old in that the older groups will be more highly selected by the fact of survival than the young. We are not able to weigh up the relative effects of these aspects of bias. However, from consideration of the work of Jarvik and Riegel in particular it seems that we can say that, in old age, deficits do occur on reasoning tests, though not on tests for which ready-made information can be used. Older adults themselves often feel inclined to challenge even such a mild statement, however. They point out that most tests on which the statement is based are timed, and that, in their own view, they have lost only *speed*, and not *power* in reasoning. Given enough time, they say, they could reason as well as they used to do.

This does not seem to be borne out in practice when complicated problems are set and no time limit is imposed. Jerome (1962) asked subjects to discover a sequence of switches which would put on a light. He found that older people were less systematic than young subjects in their search for the solution when it involved complex sequences of switching. Wetherick (1965) found that older people were less able to reason from negative instances than were younger people, even when no time limits were imposed. They often used the negative instances as though they were positive ones.

It is, however, true that older people have less 'spare capacity' with respect to speed of movement when they are asked to go as fast as possible rather than to work at their normal rate. Birren and Botwinick (1951) demonstrated this with respect to speed of writing and speed of tapping. Both are tasks where few decisions have to be made. It has been shown that, when decision making is involved, a disproportionate amount of the extra time taken by the older person is spent on the decision compared with the movement (Griew 1959). For these reasons, the imposition of a time limit may impose a strain on the older person when he is faced with a reasoning task, but the evidence is in fact equivocal and seems to depend upon the actual task involved.

We have some evidence which suggests that the strain will be greater for simple tasks than for complex ones. Lorge (1936) found that loss of speed could account for age differences in performance of the *Army Alpha* test. This consists of many simple items with a strict time limit. With a difficult task, such as items from the second half of Raven's *Matrices*, Chown (1966) found no significant difference in the use made by old and young men of the second twenty minutes spent on the test. Semeonoff and Trist (1958), with a highly intelligent and highly motivated group of subjects, found that older men (over forty-five years) made less use of an unexpected second twenty minutes on that test.

A test originally produced by Furneaux (1952) was used by Chown and Davies (1969) to examine speed and power (or level of difficulty of the problem, in Furneaux's terms) with respect to age. The test consists of a number of letter-series problems, which vary in level of difficulty as determined by the number of people in an independent sample who manage to solve each problem. Furneaux predicted that, for problems correctly solved, the log of the time to solution would be proportional to the difficulty level. A dim person would take a long time to solve an easy problem, whereas a bright person would take only a very short time. Both would take proportionally longer, in log-times, to solve a more difficult problem. Furneaux expected—and found with young servicemen as subjects—that individual performances would result in a series of parallel straight lines when log-times to solution were plotted against difficulty level.

Chown and Davies wondered whether, when older subjects were included, they might prove to take disproportionately longer over more difficult items. If loss of speed *and* loss of power occur in old age, then difficulty level plotted against log-time will give parallel lines for young and old adults. If loss of speed *only* occurs, then the lines will not be parallel. After preliminary work to establish the five levels of difficulty of the problems, ten items were given, without time limit, to 21 subjects in their twenties and thirties and to 21 subjects in their fifties and sixties. The subjects were matched for *Mill Hill Vocabulary* scores, and were above average on that test (mean 36). Time to solution for each problem was noted for each subject.

Old subjects managed to solve almost as many problems as their younger matched counterparts. (O solved 6·48, Y solved 6·95.) The old proved to take slightly longer to solve all the problems, but the gradients of the difficulty/log-time to solution lines for the two age groups did not differ from each other. Thus, speed *and* power appeared to be affected. However, the interesting finding came from an analysis of the time spent on problems to which wrong answers were eventually given. For the young subjects, at each level of difficulty, slightly longer was spent on items which were eventually wrong than items which were correctly solved. For the old subjects, a constant amount of time was spent on problems which were wrong, however 'intrinsically' easy or difficult the problems were. Thus if a test depends on many solutions to easy items, the older person *is* likely to be handicapped by his persistence at items which he cannot solve. If a test depends on solutions to difficult items, the older person, showing *less* persistence now than the young person with problems he cannot solve, does not suffer from a time handicap in relation to the young.

Conclusions

We have been concerned about the effects of age on intellectual performance. Senile changes are, it is suggested, not to be viewed as gradually evolving from the changes of normal ageing, since they do not seem to be different only in quantity from earlier deficits.

Leaving on one side the many difficulties of studying normal ageing, it does seem that the normal adult is likely to show some decline in his ability to reason logically and to work out solutions to new problems, whereas he is not likely to be hampered in his use of 'ready-made answers' or solutions which he has already worked out. Use *may* help to prolong reasoning ability—though it is difficult to be certain about this on present evidence, and there is always likely to be argument as to whether a person who has been mentally very active has not collected more ready-made answers to carry him through later life. Ill-health seems to be accompanied by a falling off in ability—especially in the case of circulatory complaints and sensory defects. There appears to be strong evidence that death is selective, and that older age groups contain more people who were originally more intelligent. This may well be an artefact of social conditions, but it means that added care must be taken in analysing and interpreting age data. Like must only be compared to like—or self to self. There are big individual differences in age effects, greater indeed as chronological age increases. Speed and power decrease together, but patterns of tackling problems may alter with respect to persistence, leading, with easy material on which the older person happens to fail, to an apparent age handicap under time-limit conditions.

As to the individual who is ageing, one suspects that he is concerned to optimise his own performance in life, just as is the young person. He can hardly be blamed if he prefers few changes in routine and casts a suspicious eye on 'improvements' which would involve new problems for him to solve. This is his way of adapting to the changes that he finds within himself. It is worth noting that the age factor in attitudinal rigidity is mainly concerned with liking for habit and suspicion of new methods (Chown 1961). Perhaps one of the most interesting questions of all is whether the older person does not sometimes *over*-adapt, and come to underestimate his own powers to cope with new situations.

R. W. Pickford

Colour vision defective art students

The problems of colour vision defects in relation to pictorial art have been raised in various ways since the time of Goethe. He realised as long ago as 1810 that such defects must have an influence on art and made coloured illustrations showing what the effect of the kind of colour vision defect we now call *protanopia*★ must be. Goethe also mentions Uccello as a painter whose works suggest colour vision defect (Goethe 1840; 1894).

Strebel discussed the case of El Greco, whom he suspected of a *pseudo-tritanopia* or yellow-blue defect due to yellowing of the optical lens with age (Strebel 1933), and Liebreich dealt with the problems of *pseudo-tritanopia* in Turner and Mulready (Liebreich 1872). He also discussed the influence of diminished sensitivity to red (*protanomaly*), an influence later called 'Liebreich's sign' of colour vision defect in an artist by Angelucci (1908).

Trevor-Roper has more recently dealt very fully with the whole subject of defective colour vision in artists (1959), and in particular mentions Constable as a possible protanomalous subject. A number of other ophthalmologists have given their attention to these problems, and probably the latest to have done so is Wirth (1968). The writer has also had the good fortune to meet several colour vision defective artists and to be successful in persuading them to undergo tests and discuss their work with him (Pickford 1964; 1965a; 1965b; 1967). It is of course essential that the suspected artist should actually be given tests of colour vision, because speculation about the possibility of defects in artists who are long dead and can never be tested is not likely to lead to decisive results, however interesting it may be.

All these studies and others not mentioned, lead to interesting and important problems about the status, competence and achievements of students in colleges of art who may have colour vision defects, and to the

---

★ For brief statements of the most frequent types of red/green colour vision defects see pages 159-63.

question of the relative efficiency of the colour vision of normal art students and non-art students. These problems, all related to educational psychology, will be dealt with briefly in what follows. Technical details which refer to colour vision and its defects, and which are fully dealt with in the books and papers mentioned in the references, have been avoided as far as possible.

It will be useful, however, to mention that about 92·5 per cent of the male population have normal colour vision, which has minor variations. These variations may affect efficiency in fine colour tasks, but would not lead to failure on any standard colour blindness test. In the remainder of the male population there are six types of red–green colour vision defect, usually called colour blindness or partial colour blindness. These are as follows: (1) *dichromatic* vision (requiring only two primaries to match all spectral hues): two types, (*a*) protanopia (about 0·5 per cent), in which the red end of the spectrum is shortened, and (*b*) deuteranopia (about 0·5 per cent), in which it is not shortened; (2) *anomalous trichromatic* vision (requiring three primaries, but the red or green in unusual proportions: four types, (*a*) simple protanomaly (about 0·5 per cent) and (*b*) extreme protanomaly (about 1·0 per cent) in which the red end of the spectrum is shortened, (*c*) simple deuteranomaly (about 2·0 per cent) and (*d*) extreme deuteranomaly (about 3·0 per cent), in which it is not shortened. These six forms of red–green defect are much less frequent in women than in men, and there are less than about 0·5 per cent of red–green defective women in our population. In addition there are yellow–blue defects and total colour blindness, both of which are very rare, occurring probably in less than 1 in 50,000 men or women. The main influence of these defects will be mentioned briefly on page 163.

Art students with normal colour vision

Several researches have indicated that normal artists, art students and colour workers have better average colour discrimination than other people with normal colour vision, when studied with various tests.

Heine and Lenz (1907) compared eighteen artists who had normal colour vision with normal subjects who were not artists, using a number of colour vision tests, including one using the colour perception spectrometer. They say that these artists had differences among themselves in colour perception similar to those found in other normal people who were not artists. In common with other people accustomed to work with colours in other ways, however, on a percentage basis on the tests, the artists gave better results than normal people who were not artists and did not work with colours.

Pierce (1934) showed that, among fifty-four staff members and students in a school of art, those who were judged by other staff members as the best colour workers were also better at his tests of colour discrimination than average colour workers of equal experience. Also those groups who had the longest experience with colours were better at the tests (Pierce 1934). The present writer tested with his anomaloscope a group of sixteen art students who had normal colour vision, thirteen of whom were women, and showed that they were a little more sensitive to red and green than the general population of the same geographical area.

These researches are being developed at the present time by a fuller study of the whole intake of students in a school of art in two successive years, compared with a group of non-art students of the same age (Cobb 1969). A preliminary report on this work failed to support the conclusion of previous work that art students have better colour vision than non-art students. However, the research is as yet incomplete, and it must be remembered that Heine and Lenz had only eighteen artists, and that these, being artists, had probably been the most successful at colour work among those of their own student peers who were not artists, while Pierce's subjects included staff members of an art college, and he compared the best colour workers with average colour workers.

It is quite possible that it may be shown conclusively that the best colour workers, staff members of schools of art and the best colourists among art students, have definitely better colour discrimination than inferior colour workers and non-art students. It would still not be known whether their superior colour discrimination was congenital, or whether it was an effect of training and practice upon colour sensitivity not congenitally better than that of the non-artists and non-colour workers. To answer this question it would be necessary to test the subjects before they underwent any training or had special experience in working with colours. Another interesting point is that good colour discrimination in the psycho-physical sense may or may not be correlated with high aesthetic or artistic sensitivity to colours.

Colour vision defectives in art schools

The writer (Pickford 1967) was able to test ten red/green colour vision defective students in four schools of art, with the consent of the principals or directors of the schools and owing to the help of friends who were teachers in those schools, or psychologists, and had been able to give the students the Ishihara test for colour blindness. These schools of art were in widely separated parts of the country—namely, Croydon, Nottingham, Aberdeen and Glasgow. After the detection with the Ishihara test of the colour vision defective students, some of whom were found in every school as stated below, the writer was able to visit the schools of art and measure the defects accurately with the Pickford/Nicolson anomaloscope (Pickford and Lakowski 1960).

This investigation showed that there were colour vision defective students in all these schools of art, but it did not give their frequency because all the students in the schools were not tested. However, it showed the relative frequencies of the different types of colour vision defectives, and it enabled the writer to study the influence of the defects on the students' work.

Nine men students were found who had red/green defective vision. These were as follows: three from Croydon and two each from Nottingham, Aberdeen and Glasgow. All brought examples of their work and discussed their problems with the writer. In addition, a Glasgow woman student had been tested by the writer some years before and found to be defective (Pickford 1951) and she was included in the study, making ten students altogether.

The frequencies of types of defect among these students did not differ significantly from those for the population as a whole. Full details of types and degrees of colour vision defects and their frequencies have been given by Pickford (1951; 1969) and Pickford and Lakowski (1960). From Croydon there were two extreme deuteranomalous and one extreme protanomalous men; from Nottingham one simple deuteranomalous and one protanope; from Aberdeen two extreme deuteranomalous; from Glasgow one simple deuteranomalous and one extreme protanomalous men, and one simple deuteranomalous woman. Since these included four out of the six usually accepted types of red-green defect, and not only the least severe, it seemed that there was no tendency for the defectives to stop studying art because of the nature or the severity of the defect. Since the schools of art were widely separated there was apparently no tendency for the defectives to be found in one school of art or one geographical area more than another, especially as all the schools of art studied had colour defectives among their students.

It is important to know how the students know about their defects. It was found that two of the men students had first discovered their defects only by taking part in this research, five had been given tests before entering the colleges of art, usually by a doctor at their previous schools

F

which were not concerned with art, and one knew of his defect by noticing errors made in daily life. The woman student did not know of her defect until tested by the writer, and then she was very surprised. It was reported by her colleagues that she was the one who generally agreed with their teacher in certain judgments about green—her most defective colour. It was said by one student that his art teacher had tried to help him by advocating a very restricted palette, although the student had a craving to enjoy the lavish use of colours in so far as he could. Another student was said to have been rejected by a different art school previously on account of his defect—he was a protanope, the most defective of them all. These points are of great interest in relation to the educational problems of how to deal with colour vision defective art students, because, as is perhaps not commonly realised, many colour vision defectives, whether students of art or not, never discover that they are defective, and others, who are tested and discovered, do not always believe the results of the tests, but continue to insist that they are normal.

The frequency of colour vision defectives in a school of art

While the research just mentioned established certain facts about the occurrence of colour defective students in schools of art, and about their kinds of defect, it did not give any definite information about their frequency among art students in those schools. In a further research, in which the writer was helped by an Honours psychology student, Donald I. A. Macleod, the students in the whole intake in two years in a school of art were studied (Pickford 1969). These included 112 men and 111 women students, who were all tested with the Ishihara test by Mr Macleod. Seven red/green defectives were found, six men and one woman. These were all re-tested with the anomaloscope, and interviewed by the writer, and all brought examples of their work and discussed their problems with him.

The frequencies of these defective men and of the defective woman in their groups did not differ to a statistically significant degree from the frequencies of red/green defectives in the general population of the same area (Pickford 1951; 1969). Also the distribution of types of defect did not differ significantly from the general distribution of types of red/green defectives in the population. There were two simple deuteranomalous men, three extreme deuteranomalous and one deuteranope; and one extreme protanomalous woman. It again appeared that there was no tendency to drop out according to degree or type of defect, and this research strongly suggested the general inference that there are as many colour vision defectives among art students as there are in the population as a whole, although it must be remembered that only a single art school was studied.

Again it is important to know how the students discovered their defect. One of the defective students had no previous knowledge of his defect, four had been tested by a doctor in their schools not concerned with art, before entering the art college, and two had found their defects through tests carried out by friends after going to the college of art.

The problems of colour vision defectives in art schools

Before giving some general observations about the problems of colour vision defectives in schools of art, it may be wise to mention very briefly the essential nature and influence of the six different kinds of red green defect under consideration. Simple deuteranomaly implies a very marked increase in the amount of green required to match a standard yellow with a mixture of red and green lights. Simple protanomaly is the opposite—a very marked increase in the amount of red required. Extreme deuteranomaly and extreme protanomaly imply very considerable red/green confusion, usually added to the defects just mentioned. Deuteranopia and protanopia imply complete red/green confusion. In addition, in all three protan defects there is extreme loss of sensitivity to red light, which makes all red colours look abnormally dark or even black.

An art student who suffers from simple deuteranomaly (or protanomaly) may find that it has little effect on his work. He will have good hue discrimination, but the scale of hues between red, yellow and green will be different for him from the normal. In the case of extreme deuteranomaly (or protanomaly) there will be very poor red/green hue discrimination, and reds, oranges, yellows and greens will tend to look alike, and so will blues, violets and purples. The deuteranope and protanope will be unable to distinguish red, orange, yellow and green, if they are of equal brightness and saturation for them, and likewise they will be unable to distinguish blue, violet and purple. The protan subjects, however, always have the advantage (or disadvantage) that reds tend to look very dark for them, but can sometimes be correctly identified in consequence.

If a student of art is not aware of his defects, and has not had unintentional practice in overcoming them, which, indeed, most will have had, then he may make outright blunders such as painting red or orange flames green, red flowers dark brown, green objects brown, and so on.

One student said he was afraid an examiner might ask him why he had painted the brown leather saddle of a bicycle green. If, however, they have had a good deal of practice and also learned, even unconsciously, how to avoid errors of this kind, then their art may not be greatly affected.

For instance, the writer knows a very good artist who is a protanope. If an observer sees one of his paintings nothing abnormal may be noticed, and within the bounds of the yellow, orange, blue, black and white colours he generally uses, his colour schemes are very clever and pleasing. He has learned to use these colours effectively, going mainly by brightness and saturation differences, and can make a picture which satisfies him as well as an observer with normal colour vision. If, however, we see a number of his works together, and also know about the nature of his defective colour vision, it is easy to see how it has influenced all his colour schemes. Although he has achieved this adaptation in his art, and has submitted to colour vision tests, he still doubts that his colour vision is abnormal, or that it has affected his art to any extent, although he confined himself to black and white work for a great part of his life for other reasons.

In addition to the influence of the colour vision defects themselves, the effects of personality and temperament interacting with them are important. A bold and extraverted student, who ignores his defects or is indifferent to them, may be able to use colours in apparently original and striking ways, but if a student is introverted and sensitive or self-conscious he may find himself involved in difficulties in trying to compensate for his defects or overcome them. Then he will be anxious about his paintings and about his examinations and he may be unable to complete his course. The greater the colour vision defects, the more difficult it will be to overcome them, and the more they will tend to make him bold if he is insensitive, or anxious if he is sensitive about them. These inferences ought to be studied by efficient researches on temperament and personality and their influence on the work of colour vision defective art students, none of which have been carried out up to the time of writing.

There is no need to conclude that all colour vision defectives should be discovered by tests and excluded from art schools or colleges. Artistic ability is not correlated with the absence of defective colour vision, and may not be correlated with exceptionally good colour vision either. Thus colour defective art students and artists often have very high artistic ability of a general kind, irrespective of their use of colour, or within the bounds of the colour uses they can make. It is interesting that the unusual and bizarre colour schemes frequently seen in much modern painting are not likely to be the outcome of defective colour vision. The colour defective is more likely to use a restricted and guarded palette, or, if he is less expert, to make plain blunders, instead of experimenting with unusual colour schemes.

Conclusion

Researches have suggested that the colour sensitivity of the best art students may be superior to that of inferior students or non-art students, but this is as yet undecided. Other researches have shown that there are as many colour vision defective students in schools of art as in the population as a whole, with no tendency to drop out because of type or degree of defect.

The colour vision defective student should be identified by adequate tests, but, instead of being rejected, he should be consulted by psychologists who understand his problems and can deal with them competently from a more clinical point of view. The most popular existing tests of colour blindness are not sensitive enough for the clinical kind of testing and guidance called for by colour defective art students. They do not give enough information about types or degree of defect. With adequate tests, it should be possible to help those who are most likely to find difficulties owing to their anxiety about their defects, and to give advice to those who are bolder and more indifferent about the possibility of troublesome errors. It is not likely that art teachers themselves would be the best at dealing with these problems because they fall within the field of clinical psychology or occupational guidance, and they also call for an understanding and knowledge of colour vision defects which would be more than is usual among art teachers.

References

The concepts of aptitude and capacity

1. FERGUSON, G. A. (1954) 'On learning and human ability.' *Canadian J. of Psych.*, **VIII**, 95-112.
2. CICERO, M. T. *De Inventione*, **I**, 27, 41.
3. CICERO, M. T. *De Inventione*, **II**, 53.
4. AQUINAS, T. *Summa Theologica*, QQ. LXXVII-LXXXVIII.
5. AQUINAS, T. *Summa Theologica*, QQ. LXXVII.
6. AQUINAS, T. *Summa Theologica*, Q. LXXIX.
7. CHAUCER, G. *Astrolabe*, 1.
8. SHAKESPEARE, W. *Troilus and Cressida*, I, iii, 179.
9. HAMILTON, W. *Lectures on Metaphysics*, **II**, 13 and 23.
10. HAMILTON, W. *Lectures on Metaphysics*, **II**, 227.
11. BACON, F. *Novum Organum*, LXIII.
12. HOBBES, T. *De Corpore*, Works, I, 132.
13. LOCKE, J. *Essay on Human Understanding*, **II**, 1.
14. LOCKE, J. *Essay on Human Understanding*, **II**, xxi.
15. HELVETIUS, C. A. (1758) *De l'esprit*.
16. JACOTOT, J. (1823) *Enseignement universal*, p. 198.
17. HERBART, J. F. (1816) *Lehrbuch zur Psychologie*, **III**, 152.
18. TAINE, H. (1871) *On Intelligence*, English tr., Preface.
19. TAINE, H. (1871) *On Intelligence*, p. 71.
20. STOUT, G. F. (1896) *Analytical Psychology*, **I**, 18.
21. WARD, J. (1918) *Psychological Principles*, p. 60 (based on Ward's Encyclopedia Britannica article of 1888). London: Cambridge University Press.
22. SULLY, J. (1884) *Outlines of Psychology*, p. 32.
23. SPURZHEIM, J. G. (1908 rep., originally 1833) *Phrenology*, p. 40. Philadelphia: Lippincott.
24. ALLPORT, G. (1937) *Personality*, p. 82. New York: Holt. See also SPOERL, H. G. (1936) 'Faculties or traits: the solution of F. J. Gall,' in *Character and Personality*, IV, 216-31.
25. BAILEY, S. (1855-63) *Letters on the Human Mind*, **II**, 206.
26. ESQUIROL, J. E. D. (1838) 'Des maladies mentales considérées sous les rapports médical, hygiénique et médico-légal.'

27. MOREAU DE TOURS (1830) 'De l'influence du physique relativement au désordre des facultés intellectuelles.'
28. MOREL, B. A. (1857) Traité des dégénérescences physiques, intellectuelles et morales de l'espèce homme.'
29. DRYDEN, J. (1631-1700) 'Great wits are sure to madness near allied, and thin partitions do their bounds divide.' *Absalom and Achitophel.*
30. GALTON, F. (1865) 'Hereditary talent and character.' In *Macmillan's Magazine,* **XII,** 157-66, 318-27.
31. GALTON, F. (1869) *Hereditary Genius,* p. 17.
32. BINET, A. and HENRI, V. (1895) 'La psychologie individuelle.' In *L'Année psychologique,* **II,** 411-65.
33. SPEARMAN, C. E. (1937) *Psychology down the Ages,* **I,** ch. XI. London: Macmillan.
34. SPEARMAN, C. E. (1927) *The Abilities of Man,* Preface. London: Macmillan.
35. VERNON, P.E. (1950) *The Structure of Human Abilities,* p. 8. London: Methuen.
36. SPEARMAN, C. E. (1937) *Psychology down the Ages,* **II.** London: Macmillan.
37. BUTCHER, H. J. (1968) *Human Intelligence.* London: Methuen.
38. RYLE, G. (1949) *The Concept of Mind.* London: Hutchinson.
39. MILES, T. R. (1957) 'On defining intelligence.' *Brit. J. educ. Psych.,* **27,** 153-65.
40. BURT, C. L. (1949) 'The structure of the mind.' *Brit. J. educ. Psych.,* **19,** 100-111.
41. WISEMAN, S. (1967) (ed.) *Intelligence and Ability,* Introduction, p. 15. Harmondsworth, Middlesex: Penguin.

Consistency and variability in the growth of human characteristics

ALTUS, W. D. (1966) 'Birth order and its sequelae.' *Science,* **151,** 44-9.
ANDERSON, J. E. (1963) *Experience and Behaviour in Early Childhood and the Adjustment of the same Persons as Adults.* University of Minnesota, Institute of Child Development.
BALLER, W. R., CHARLES, D. C. and MILLER, E. L. (1967) 'Mid-life attainment of the mentally retarded: a longitudinal study.' *Genet. Psychol. Monogr.,* **75,** 235-329.
BEREITER, C. and ENGELMANN, S. (1966) *Teaching Disadvantaged Children in the Preschool.* Englewood Cliffs, N.J.: Prentice-Hall.
BLOOM, B. S. (1964) *Stability and Change in Human Characteristics.* London: John Wiley.
BRADLEY, R. W. (1968) 'Birth order and school related behavior.' *Psychol. Bull.,* **70,** 45-51.
CHARLES, D. C. and JAMES, S. T. (1964) 'Stability of average intelligence.' *J. genet. Psychol.,* **105,** 105-111.
CHITTENDEN, E. A., FOAN, M. W. and ZWEIL, D. M. (1968) 'School achievement of first and second born children.' *Child Dev.,* **39,** 1223-8.

CLARKE, A. D. B. (1968) 'Learning and human development—the forty-second Maudsley Lecture.' *Br. J. Psychiat.*, **114**, 1061-77.

CLARKE, A. D. B. (1969) *Recent Advances in the Study of Subnormality*. London: NAMH.

CLARKE, A. D. B. (1970) 'Problems in assessing the effects of early experience.' *Advancement of Science*, **26**, 379-85.

CLARKE, A. D. B. and CLARKE, A. M. (1954) 'Cognitive changes in the feeble minded.' *Br. J. Psychol.*, **45**, 173-9.

CLARKE, A. D. B., CLARKE, A. M. and REIMAN, S. (1958) 'Cognitive and social changes in the feeble minded—three further studies.' *Br. J. Psychol.*, **49**, 144-57.

DEARBORN, W. F. and ROTHNEY, J. M. W. (1941) *Predicting the Child's Development*. Cambridge, Mass.: Sci-Art Publication.

DOUGLAS, J. W. B. (1964) *The Home and the School*. London: MacGibbon and Kee.

DOUGLAS, J. W. B., ROSS, J. M. and SIMPSON, H. R. (1968) *All our Future*. London: Peter Davies.

FELD, S. C. (1967) 'Longitudinal study of the origins of achievement strivings.' *J. pers. soc. Psychol.*, **7**, 408-14.

GRAY, S. and KLAUS, R. A. (1970) 'The early training project: a seventh-year report.' *Child Dev.*, **41**, 909-24.

HEBER, R. and GARBER, H. (1971) 'An experiment in the prevention of "Cultural-Familial" mental retardation.' *Proc. Second Congr. Internat. Assoc. scientif. Stud. ment. Defic*, 31-5. Amsterdam: Swets and Zeitlinger.

HOCKEY, S. W. (1968) 'Intelligence, Common Entrance and the General Certificate of Education.' *Br. J. educ. Psychol.*, **38**, 140-7.

HONZIK, M. P., MACFARLANE, J. W. and ALLEN, L. (1948) 'The stability of mental test performance between two and eighteen years.' *J. exp. Educ.*, **17**, 309-24.

HUSEN, T. (1951) 'The influence of schooling upon IQ.' *Theoria*, **17**, 61-88.

JENSEN, A. R. (1969) 'How much can we boost IQ and scholastic achievement?' *Harvard educ. Rev.*, **39**(1), 123.

KAGAN, J. and MOSS, H. A. (1959) 'Stability and validity of achievement fantasy.' *J. abnorm. soc. Psychol.*, **58**, 357-64.

KAGAN, J. and MOSS, H. A. (1962) *Birth to Maturity*. London: John Wiley.

LIVSON, N. and PESKIN, H. (1967) 'Prediction of adult psychological health in a longitudinal study.' *J. abnorm. Psychol.*, **72**, 509-18.

MOSS, H. A. and KAGAN, J. (1961) 'Stability of achievement and recognition seeking behaviors from early childhood through adulthood.' *J. abnorm. soc. Psychol.*, **62**, 504-13.

ODEN, M. H. (1968) 'The fulfilment of promise: 40-year follow-up of the Terman Gifted Group.' *Genet. Psychol. Monogr.*, **77**, 3-93.

PIDGEON, D. A. (1970) *Expectation and Pupil Performance*. Slough: NFER.

ROBINS, L. N. (1966) *Deviant Children Grown Up*. Baltimore: Williams and Wilkins.

SCHACHTER, S. (1963) 'Birth order, eminence and higher education.' *Am. sociol. Rev.*, **28**, 757-68.

SHAPIRO, M. B. (1951) 'An experimental approach to diagnostic testing.' *J. ment. Sci.*, **97**, 748-64.

SONTAG, L. W., BAKER, C. T. and NELSON, V. C. (1958) 'Mental growth and personality development: a longitudinal study.' *Monogr. Soc. Res. Child Dev.*, **23** (68).

SUNDBY, H. S. and KREYBURG, P. C. (1969) *Prognosis in Child Psychiatry*. Baltimore: Williams and Wilkins.

THOMAS, A., CHESS, S. and BIRCH, H. G. (1969) *Temperament and Behaviour Disorders in Children*. London: University of London Press.

VERNON, P. E. (1955) 'Presidential address: the psychology of intelligence and *g*.' *Bull. Br. Psychol. Soc.*, **26**, 1-14.

VERNON, P. E. (1964) *Personality Assessment: A Critical Survey*. London: Methuen.

VERNON, P. E. (1970) 'Intelligence'. In DOCKRELL, W. B. (ed.) *On Intelligence*. London: Methuen.

WISEMAN, S. and START, K. B. (1965) 'A follow-up of teachers five years after completing their training.' *Br. J. educ. Psychol.*, **35**, 342-61.

Environmental handicap and the teacher

BEREITER, C. and ENGELMANN, S. (1966) *Teaching Disadvantaged Children in the Pre-School*. New Jersey: Prentice Hall.

BURSTALL, C. (1968) *French from Eight*. Slough: NFER.

BURT, C. (1937) *The Backward Child*. London: University of London Press.

BURT, C. (1943) 'Ability and income.' *Br. J. educ. Psychol.*, **13**, 83-98.

CHAUNCEY, M. R. (1929) 'Relation of the home factor to achievement and intelligence test scores.' *J. educ. Res.*, **20**, 88-90.

Dept. of Education and Science (1967) *Children and their Primary Schools* (Plowden Report). London: HMSO.

DOUGLAS, J. W. B. (1964) *The Home and the School*. London: McGibbon and Kee.

FLOUD, J. E., HALSEY, A. H. and MARTIN, F. M. (1957) *Social Class and Educational Opportunity*. London: Heinemann.

FRASER, E. D. (1959) *Home Environment and the School*. London: London University Press.

GLASS, D. V. (ed.) (1954) *Social Mobility in Britain*. London: Routledge and Kegan Paul.

HALSEY, A. H. and GARDNER, L. (1953) 'Selection for secondary education and achievement.' *Br. J. Sociol.*, **4**, 60-75.

HAYNES, J. (1971) *Educational Assessment of Immigrant Pupils*. Slough: NFER.

JAHODA, G. (1970) 'A cross-cultural perspective in Psychology.' *Advancement of Science*, 27.

JENSEN, A. R. (1969) 'How much can we boost IQ and scholastic achievement?' *Harvard educ. Rev.*, **39**, 1-123.

LESSER, G. S., FIFER, G. and CLARK, D. M. (1965) 'Mental abilities of children from different social-class and cultural groups.' *Monograph for Soc. for Res. in Child Dev.* No. 102. Vol. **30**, No. 4.

LUNN, J. BARKER (1970) *Streaming in the Primary School*. Slough: NFER.

MAXWELL, J. (1953) *Social Implications of the 1947 Scottish Mental Survey*. Publications of the Scottish Council for Research in Education. London: University of London Press.

Ministry of Education (1954) *Early Leaving*. London: HMSO.

PEAKER, G. F. (1971) *The Plowden Follow-up*. (In the press.)

PIDGEON, D. A. (1970) *Expectation and Pupil Performance*. Slough: NFER.

QUIGLEY, H. (1971) 'Reactions of eleven nursery teachers and assistants to the Peabody Language Development Kit.' *Br. J. educ. Psychol*, **41**, 155-62.

Schools Council (1970) *Cross'd with Adversity*. Working Paper 27. London: Evans/Methuen Educational.

SHAW, D. C. (1943) 'Relation of socio-economic status to educational achievement in grades 4-8.' *J. Educ. Res.*, **37**, 193-201.

SPINLEY, B. M. (1953) *The Deprived and the Privileged*. London: Routledge and Kegan Paul.

TOWNSEND, H. E. R. (1970) 'The In-Service Training of Teachers in Primary and Secondary Schools.' In Dept. of Educ. and Sci. *Statistics of Education* Special Series No. 2. London: HMSO.

TOWNSEND, H. E. R. (1971) *Multiracial Schools in England Part I: LEA Arrangements*. (In the press.) Slough: NFER.

VERNON, P. E. (1969) *Intelligence and Cultural Environment*. London: Methuen.

WISEMAN, S. (1964) *Education and Environment*. Manchester: Manchester University Press.

Growth of formal operational thinking

BART, E. (1970) 'The factor structure of formal operations.' *Br. J. educ. Psychol.*, **41**, 70-7.

BEILIN, H. (1969) 'Stimulus and Cognitive Transformation in Conservation.' In ELKIND, D. and FLAVELL, J. H. (eds) *Studies in Cognitive Development*. New York: Oxford University Press.

GOLDMAN, R. J. (1964) *Religious Thinking from Childhood to Adolescence*. London: Routledge and Kegan Paul.

HALLAM, R. N. (1967) 'Logical thinking in history.' *Educ. Rev.*, **19**, 183-202.

HUGHES, M. M. (1965) 'A four year longitudinal study of the growth of logical thinking in a group of secondary modern schoolboys.' M.Ed. thesis, University of Leeds.

INHELDER, B. and PIAGET, J. (1958) *The Growth of Logical Thinking.* London: Routledge and Kegan Paul.

JACKSON, S. (1965) 'The growth of logical thinking in normal and subnormal children.' *Br. J. educ. Psychol.*, **35**, 255-58.

KIMBALL, R. L. (1968) *A Background Concept Study in Malawi.* Domasi: Science Centre.

LOVELL, K. (1961) 'A follow-up study of Inhelder and Piaget's *The Growth of Logical Thinking.*' *Br. J. Psychol.*, **52**, 142-53.

LOVELL, K. and BUTTERWORTH, I. B. (1966) 'Abilities underlying the understanding of proportionality.' *Mathematics Teaching*, **37**, 5-9.

LOVELL, K. and SHIELDS, J. B. (1967) 'Some aspects of a study of the gifted child.' *Br. J. educ. Psychol.*, **37**, 201-8.

LUNZER, E. A. (1965) 'Problems of formal reasoning in test situations.' In MUSSEN, P. H. (ed.) 'European research in cognitive development.' *Monogr. Soc. Res. Child Dev.*, Vol. **30**, No. 2.

LUNZER, E. A. (1968) 'Formal reasoning.' In LUNZER, E. A. and MORRIS, J. F. (eds) *Development in Learning 2.* London: Staples.

PELUFFO, N. (1967) 'Culture and cognitive problems.' *Int. J. Psychol.*, **2**, 187-198.

PIAGET, J. et al. (1968) *Épistémologie et Psychologie de la Function.* Paris: Presses Universitaires de France.

SHEPLER, J. L. (1969) *A Study of Parts of the Development of a Unit in Probability and Statistics for the Elementary School.* Madison: The University of Wisconsin Research and Development Center for Cognitive Learning.

STEFFE, L. P. and PARR, R. B. (1968) *The Development of the Concepts of Ratio and Fraction in the Fourth, Fifth and Sixth Years of the Elementary School.* Madison: The University of Wisconsin Research and Development Center for Cognitive Learning.

TANNER, J. M. and INHELDER, B. (1960) (eds) *Discussions on Child Development 4.* London: Tavistock Publications.

VERNON, P. E. (1969) *Intelligence and Cultural Environment.* London: Methuen.

Divergent thinking and creativity

BIRKIN, T. A. (1970) 'Dimensions of creativity in elementary school children: parsimonious models of divergent thinking data.' Unpublished manuscript.

BOERSMA, F. J. and O'BRYAN, K. (1968) 'An investigation of the relationship between creativity and intelligence under two conditions of testing.' *J. Personality*, **36**, 341-8.

CALLISTER, J. (1970) 'Individual differences in cognitive style: preference for complexity-simplicity.' M.Sc. thesis, University of Aston.

CAMERON, L. (1968) 'Intelligence, creativity and the English examination.' *Scot. educ. Studies*, **1**, 55-60.

CHILD, D. and SMITHERS, A. (1971) 'Some cognitive and affective factors in subject choice.' *Res. in Educ.*, **5**, 1-9.

CHRISTIE, T. (1969) 'Contrary imaginations at Keele: an alternative interpretation.' *Univ. Quart.*, **24**, 91-2.

CLARKE, D. F. (1968) 'Some aspects of creative thinking abilities in British schoolchildren.' Ph.D. thesis, University of Reading.

CRONBACH, L. J. (1968) ' "Intelligence? Creativity?" A parsimonious reinterpretation of the Wallach-Kogan data.' *Am. educ. Res. J.*, **5**, 491-512.

CROPLEY, A. J. (1968) 'A note on the Wallach-Kogan tests of creativity.' *Br. J. educ. Psychol.*, **38**, 197-200.

DACEY, J., MADAUS, G. F. and ALLEN, A. (1969) 'The relationship of creativity and intelligence in Irish adolescents.' *Br. J. educ. Psychol.*, **39**, 261-6.

DI SCIPIO, W. J. (1968) 'Verbal fluency, originality and vocational choice as measures of personality and arts-science specialisation.' Ph.D. thesis, University of London.

ELKIND, D., DEBLINGER, J. and ADLER, D. (1970) 'Motivation and creativity: the context effect.' *Am. educ. Res. J.*, **7**, 351-67.

FEE, F. (1968) 'An alternative to Ward's factor analysis of Wallach and Kogan's "creativity" correlations.' *Br. J. educ. Psychol.*, **38**, 319-21.

FURSE-ROBERTS, E. (1966) 'An investigation of the interrelationships among tests of creativity and of ability in secondary school children.' Unpublished thesis, Belfast, Queen's University.

GETZELS, J. W. and JACKSON, P. W. (1962) *Creativity and Intelligence.* New York: Wiley.

GUY, E. D. W. (1965) 'Creativity, intelligence, high level reasoning and academic performance.' Unpublished thesis, Belfast, Queen's University.

HADDON, F. A. and LYTTON, H. (1968) 'Thinking approach and the development of divergent thinking abilities in primary schools.' *Br. J. educ. Psychol.*, **38**, 171-80.

HARTLEY, J. and BEASLEY, N. (1969) 'Contrary imaginations at Keele.' *Univ. Quart.*, **23**, 467-71.

HASAN, P. and BUTCHER, H. J. (1966) 'Creativity and intelligence: a partial replication with Scottish children of Getzels and Jackson's study.' *Br. J. Psychol.*, **57**, 129-35.

HEIM, A. (1970) *Intelligence and Personality.* Harmondsworth, Middlesex: Penguin.

HUDSON, L. (1966) *Contrary Imaginations.* London: Methuen.

HUDSON, L. (1968) *Frames of Mind.* London: Methuen.

HUTCHINGS, D. and POLE, K. (1968) 'The post-graduate intentions of science students.' *Univ. Quart.*, **22**, 167-75.

IRVINE, S. R. (1967) 'A study of the problem-solving abilities of children of high and low creative potential.' Unpublished thesis, Belfast, Queen's University.

JOYCE, C. R. B. and HUDSON, L. (1968) 'Student style and teacher style: an experimental study.' *Br. J. med. Educ.*, **2**, 28-32.

KUHN, T. S. (1962) *The Structure of Scientific Revolutions.* Chicago University Press.

LYTTON, H. and COTTON, A. C. (1969) 'Divergent thinking abilities in secondary schools.' *Br. J. educ. Psychol.*, **39**, 188-90.

MCHENRY, R. E. and SHOUKSMITH, G. A. (1970) 'Creativity, visual imagination and suggestibility: their relationship in a group of ten-year-old children.' *Br. J. educ. Psychol.*, **40**, 154-60.

MARINO, C. J. (1968) 'Creativity and conformity in school children as influenced by religious affiliation and type of school attended.' Ph.D. thesis, University of Edinburgh.

MARINO, C. J. (1971) 'Cross-national comparisons of Catholic-Protestant creativity differences.' *Br. J. soc. clin. Psychol.*, **10**, 132-7.

MOORE, F. E. (1966) 'The relevance of divergent thinking and neuroticism to achievement.' Unpublished thesis, Belfast, Queen's University.

NUTTALL, D. (1971) 'Modes of thinking and their measurement.' Ph.D. thesis, University of Cambridge.

OGILVIE, E. (1970) 'Creativity, intelligence and concept development.' Ph.D. thesis, University of Southampton.

PETERS, R. S. (1968) (ed.) *Perspectives on Plowden*. London: Routledge and Kegan Paul.

POLE, K. E. (1969) 'A study of techniques for measuring creative ability and the development and validation of creativity tests for highly intelligent subjects.' B.Litt. thesis, University of Oxford.

ROGERS, E. M. (1962) *Diffusion of Innovations*. London: Collier-Macmillan.

SHAPIRO, R. J. (1968) 'Creative research scientists.' *Psychol. Africana, Monogr. Suppl.* No. 4.

SHOUKSMITH, G. (1970) *Intelligence, Creativity and Cognitive Style*. London: Batsford.

TURNBULL, G. H. (1970) 'The development of originality in young children.' Ph.D. thesis, University of Strathclyde.

VERNON, P. E. (1969) *Intelligence and Cultural Environment*. London: Methuen.

VERNON, P. E. (1970) (ed.) *Creativity*. Harmondsworth, Middlesex: Penguin.

WALLACH, M. A. and KOGAN, N. (1965) *Modes of Thinking in Young Children*. New York: Holt, Rinehart and Winston.

WALLACH, M. A. and WING, C. W. (1969) *The Talented Student*. New York: Holt, Rinehart and Winston.

WHITE, J. (1968) 'Creativity and education.' *Br. J. educ. Studies*, **17**, 123-7.

WOOD, R. and SKURNIK, L. S. (1969) *Item Banking*. Slough: National Foundation for Education Research.

Personality and learning

AMSEL, A. (1950) 'The effect upon level of consummatory response of the addition of anxiety to a motivational complex. *J. exp. Psychol.*, **40**, 109-15.

AMSEL, A. and MALTZMAN, I. (1950) 'The effect upon generalised drive strength of emotionality as inferred from the level of consummatory response.' *J. exp. Psychol.*, **40**, 563-9.

AXELROD, H. S., COWEN, E. L. and HEILITZER, F. (1956) 'The correlates of manifest anxiety in style and image learning.' *J. exp. Psychol.*, **51**, 131-8.

BESCH, N. F. (1959) 'Paired associate learning as a function of anxiety level and shock.' *J. Personality*, **27**, 116-24.

CASTANEDA, A. (1956) 'Effects of stress on complex learning and performance.' *J. exp. Psychol.*, **52**, 9-12.

CASTANEDA, A. (1961) 'Supplementary report: differential position habits and anxiety in children as determinants of performance in learning.' *J. exp. Psychol.*, **61**, 257-8.

CASTANEDA, A. and LIPSITT, L. P. (1959) 'Relation of stress and differential position habits to performance in motor learning.' *J.exp. Psychol.* **57**, 25-30.

CASTANEDA, A., and PALERMO, D. S. (1955) 'Psychomotor performance as a function of amount of training and stress.' *J. exp. Psychol.*, **50**, 175-9.

CASTANEDA, A., PALERMO, D. S. and MCCANDLESS, B. R. (1956) 'Complex learning and performance as a function of anxiety in children and task difficulty.' *Child Dev.*, **27**, 327-32.

CHILD, I. L. (1954) 'Personality.' *Ann. Rev. Psychol.*, **5**, 149-70.

CHILES, W. D. (1958) 'Effects of shock-induced stress on verbal performance.' *J. exp. Psychol.*, **56**, 159-65.

CLARK, R. E. (1962) 'The role of drive (time stress) in complex learning: an emphasis on prelearning phenomena.' *J. exp. Psychol.*, **63**, 57-61.

CRAVENS, R. W. and RENNER, K. E. (1970) 'Conditioned appetitive drive states.' *Psychol. Bull.*, **73**, 212-20.

DAVIDSON, W. Z., ANDREWS, T. G. and ROSS, S. (1956) 'Effects of stress and anxiety on continuous high-speed colour naming.' *J.exp.Psychol.*, **52**, 13-17.

DEESE, J., LAZARUS, R. S. and KEENAN, J. (1953) 'Anxiety, anxiety reduction, and stress in learning.' *J. exp. Psychol.*, **46**, 55-60.

DILLON, R. F. and REID, L. S. (1969) 'Short-term memory as a function of information processing during the retention interval.' *J. exp. Psychol.*, **81**, 261-9.

EYSENCK, H. J. (1957) *The Dynamics of Anxiety and Hysteria.* London: Routledge and Kegan Paul.

EYSENCK, H. J. (1967) *The Biological Basis of Personality.* Springfield: C. C. Thomas.

EYSENCK, H. J. (1971) 'Personality, learning and "anxiety".' In H. J. EYSENCK (ed.) *Handbook of Abnormal Psychology*, 2nd Edition. London: Pitman.

EYSENCK, H. J. and EYSENCK, S. B. G. (eds) (1969) *Personality Structure and Measurement.* London: Routledge and Kegan Paul.

EYSENCK, H. J. and COOKSON, D. (1969) 'Personality in primary school-children: I. Ability and achievement.' *Br. J. educ. Psychol.*, **39**, 109-22.

FARBER, I. E. and SPENCE, K. W. (1953) 'Complex learning and conditioning as a function of anxiety.' *J. exp. Psychol.*, **45**, 120-5.

GEBHARDT, R. (1966) Unpublished work. Düsseldorf: Psychol. Inst.

GORDON, W. M., and BERLYNE, D. E. (1954) 'Drive-level flexibility in paired-associate nonsense syllable learning.' *Quart. J. exp. Psychol.*, 6, 181-5.

GRANT, D. K. (1969) 'The relationship between personality and short-term memory.' Natal, Durban: Unpublished thesis.

HILGARD, E. R. (1956) *Theories of Learning* (2nd Edition). New York: Appleton-Century-Crofts.

HOWARTH, E. (1963) 'Some laboratory measures of extraversion-introversion.' *Percept. mot. Skills*, 17, 55-60.

HOWARTH, E. (1969a) 'Extraversion and increased interference in paired-associate learning.' *Percept. mot. Skills*, 29, 403-6.

HOWARTH, E. (1969b) 'Personality differences in serial learning under distraction.' *Percept. mot. Skills*, 28, 379-82.

HOWARTH, E. and EYSENCK, H. J. (1968) 'Extraversion, arousal, and paired-associate recall. *J. exp. Res. in Person.*, 3, 114-16.

HUGHES, J. B., SPRAGUE, J. L. and BENDIG, A. W. (1954) 'Anxiety level, response alteration, and performance in serial learning.' *J. Psychol.*, 38, 421-6.

JENSEN, A. (1962) 'Extraversion, neuroticism and serial learning.' *Acta psychol.*, 20, 69-77.

JENSEN, A. (1964) *Individual Differences in Learning: Interference Factor*. U.S. Dept. Health, Educ. & Welfare, Project Report No. 1867.

JOHN, E. R. (1967) *Mechanism of Memory*. New York: Academic Press.

KAMIN, L. J. and FEDORCHAK, O. (1957) 'The Taylor scale, hunger and verbal learning.' *Can. J. Psychol.*, 11, 212-18.

KATAHN, M. (1964) 'Effects of anxiety (drive) on the acquisition and avoidance of a dominant intratask response.' *J. Personality*, 32, 642-50.

KATAHN, M. and LYDA, L. L. (1966) 'Anxiety and the learning of responses varying in initial rank in the response hierarchy.' *J. Personality*, 34, 287-99.

KATCHMAR, L. T., ROSS, S. and ANDREWS, T. G. (1958) 'Effects of stress and anxiety on performance of a complex verbal-coding task.' *J. exp. Psychol.*, 55, 559-64.

LAZARUS, R. S., DEESE, J. and HAMILTON, R. (1954) 'Anxiety and stress in learning: the role of intraserial duplication.' *J. exp. Psychol.*, 47, 111-14.

LEE, C. (1961) 'The effects of anxiety level and shock as a paired-associate verbal task.' *J. exp. Psychol.*, 61, 213-17.

LOVAAS, O. I. (1960) 'The relationship of induced muscular tension, tension level, and manifest anxiety in learning.' *J. exp. Psychol.*, 59, 145-52.

LUCAS, J. P. (1952) 'The interactive effects of anxiety, failure, and intraserial duplication.' *Am. J. Psychol.*, 65, 59-66.

MACCORQUODALE, K. and MEEHL, P. E. (1954) 'Edward C. Tolman.' In W. K. ESTES *et al.* (eds) *Modern Learning Theory*. New York: Appleton-Century-Crofts.

MCLAUGHLIN, R. J. and EYSENCK, H. J. (1967) 'Extraversion, neuroticism and paired-associate learning.' *J. exp. Res. in Person.*, 2, 128-32.

MCLEAN, P. D. (1968) 'Paired-associate learning as a function of recall interval, personality and arousal.' London: Unpublished Ph.D. thesis.

MALMO, R. B., and AMSEL, A. (1948) 'Anxiety-produced interference in serial rote learning with observations on rote learning after partial frontal lobectomy.' *J. exp. Psychol.*, **38**, 440-54.

MATARAZZO J. P., ULETT, A. A. and SASLOV, G. (1955) 'Human maze performance on a function of increasing levels of anxiety.' *J. gen. Psychol.*, **43**, 79-95.

MILLER, N. E. (1948) 'Studies of fear as an acquirable drive: 5. Fear as motivation and fear-reduction as reinforcement in the learning of new responses.' *J. exp. Psychol.*, **38**, 89-101.

MILLER, N. E. (1951) 'Learnable drives and rewards.' In S. S. SHEVENS (ed.) *Handbook of Experimental Psychology*. New York: Wiley.

MONTAGUE, E. K. (1953) 'The role of anxiety in serial rote learning.' *J. exp. Psychol.*, **45**, 91-6.

NICHOLSON, W. M. (1958) 'The influence of anxiety upon learning: interference or drive increment?' *J. Personality*, **26**, 303-19.

RAYMOND, C. K. (1953) 'Anxiety and task as determinants of verbal performance.' *J. exp. Psychol.*, **46**, 120-4.

SARASON, I. G. (1956) 'Effect of anxiety, motivational instructions, and failure on serial learning.' *J. exp. Psychol.*, **51**, 253-60.

SARASON, I. G. (1957a) 'Effect of anxiety and two kinds of motivating instructions on verbal learning.' *J. abnorm. soc. Psychol.*, **57**, 166-71.

SARASON, I. G. (1957b) 'The effect of anxiety and two kinds of failure on serial learning.' *J. Personality*, **25**, 383-91.

SARASON, I. G. (1961) 'The effect of anxiety and threat on the solution of a difficult task.' *J. abnorm. soc. Psychol.*, **62**, 165-8.

SARASON, I. G., and PALOLA, E. G. (1960) 'The relationship of test and general anxiety, difficulty of task, and experimental instructions to performance.' *J. exp. Psychol.*, **59**, 185-91.

SHANMUGAN, T. E. and SANTHANAM, M. C. (1964) 'Personality differences in serial learning when interference is presented at the marginal visual level.' *J. Ind. Acad. Appl. Psychol.*, **1**, 25-8.

SIEGMAN, A. W. (1957) 'Some relationships of anxiety and introversion-extraversion to serial learning.' Ann Arbor, Michigan: Unpublished Ph.D. thesis.

SILVERMAN, R. E., and BLITZ, B. (1956) 'Learning and two kinds of anxiety.' *J. abnorm. soc. Psychol.*, **52**, 301-3.

SPENCE, J. T. and SPENCE, K. V. (1966) 'The motivational components of manifest anxiety: drive and drive stimuli.' In C. D. SPIELBERGER (ed.) *Anxiety and Behaviour*. London: Academic Press.

SPENCE, K. V. (1958) 'A theory of emotionally based drive (D) and its relation to performance in simple learning situations.' *Am. Psychol.*, **13**, 131-41.

SPENCE, K. V., FARBER, I. E. and MCFANN, H. H. (1956) 'The relation of anxiety (drive) level to performance in occupational and non-occupational paired-associates learning.' *J. exp. Psychol.*, **52**, 296-305.

SPENCE, K. V., TAYLOR, J. and KETCHEL, R. (1956) 'Anxiety (drive) level and degree of competition in paired-associates learning.' *J. exp. Psychol.*, **52**, 306-10.

SPIELBERGER, C. D. and SMITH, L. H. (1966) 'Anxiety (drive), stress and serial-position effects in serial-verbal learning.' *J. exp. Psychol.*, **72**, 585-95.

STANDISH, R. R. and CHAMPION, R. A. (1960) 'Task difficulty and drive in verbal learning.' *J. exp. Psychol.*, **59**, 361-5.

TALLAND, G. A. (1967) 'Short-term memory with interpolated activity.' *J. verb. Learn. verb. Behav.*, **6**, 144-50.

TAYLOR, J. A. (1958) 'The effects of anxiety level and psychological stress in verbal·learning.' *J. abnorm. soc. Psychol.*, **57**, 55-60.

TAYLOR, J. A. and CHAPMAN, J. P. (1955) 'Anxiety and the learning of paired-associates.' *Am. J. Psychol.*, **68**, 671.

TAYLOR, J. A. and SPENCE, K. V. (1952) 'The relationship of anxiety level to performance in serial learning.' *J. exp. Psychol.*, **44**, 61-4.

WALKER, E. L. (1958) 'Action decrement and its relation to learning.' *Psychol. Rev.*, **65**, 129-42.

WALKER, E. L. and TARTE, R. D. (1963) 'Memory storage as a function of arousal and time with homogeneous and heterogeneous tests.' *J. verb. Learn. verb. Behav.*, **2**, 113-19.

WHITLOCK, R. V. (1969) 'A further study of the effects of emotional arousal in learning.' Univ. London: Unpublished Ph.D. thesis.

WILLOUGHBY, R. H. (1967) 'Emotionality and performance in competitional and non-competitional paired-associates.' *Psychol. Rep.*, **20**, 659-62.

Mental and personality correlates of motor abilities

BLOOMERS, C. et al. (1955) 'The organismic age concept.' *J. educ. Psychol.*, **46**.

COWELL, CHARLES C. and FRANCE, W. (1963) *Philosophy and Principles of Physical Education.* New York: Prentice-Hall.

FLEISHMAN, E. (1964) *The Structure and Measurement of Physical Fitness.* New York: Prentice-Hall.

HUMPHREY, J. H. (1962) 'A pilot study of the use of physical education as a learning medium in the development of language arts concepts in third grade children.' *Res. Quart.*, **31**(1).

HUMPHREY, J. H. (1966) 'An exploratory study of active games in learning of number concepts by first grade boys and girls.' *Perceptual and Motor Skills*, **23**.

HUMPHREY, J. H. (1967) 'Academic skill and concept development through motor activity.' *Academy Papers No. 1, The American Academy of Physical Education.* University of Arizona.

HUSMAN, B. (1969) 'Sport and personality dynamics.' *Proc. N.C.P.E.M.*, University of Minnesota.

ISMAIL, A. H. (1967) 'The effects of a well organised physical education programme on intellectual performance.' *Research in Physical Education*, **1**(2).

ISMAIL, A. H. and GRUBER, J. (1965) 'Utilization of motor aptitude tests in predicting academic achievement.' *Proc. 1st International Congress of Sports Psychology*, Rome.

ISMAIL, A. H. and GRUBER, J. (1967) *Integrated Developments: Motor Aptitude and Intellectual Performance*. New York: Charles E. Merrill.

ISMAIL, A. H., KANE, J. and KIRKENDALL, D. (1969) 'Relationships among intellectual and non-intellectual variables.' *Res. Quart.*, **40**(1).

KANE, J. E. (1966) 'Personality description of soccer ability.' *Research in Physical Education*, **1**(1).

KANE, J. E. (1968) 'Personality and physical ability.' In KENYON, G. (ed.) *Proc. International Congress of Sports Psychology*, Washington, Athletic Institute.

KANE, J. E. (1970) 'Correlational strategies for identifying the association between the personality and physical ability domains.' *Proc. Integrated Development Symposium*. Indiana University, Bloomington.

KIRKENDALL, D. (1968) *The Relationships Among Motor, Intellectual and Personality Domains of Development in Pre-Adolescent Children*. Ph.D. Dissertation. University of Purdue.

KLAUSMEIER, H. J. et al. (1959). *An Analysis of Learning Efficiency in Arithmetic of Mentally Retarded Children in Comparison with Children of Average and High Intelligence*. Univ. of Wisconsin.

KROLL, W. (1967) 'Sixteen personality factor profile of collegiate wrestlers.' *Res. Quart.*, **38**.

KROLL, W. and PETERSEN, K. (1965) 'Personality factor profiles of collegiate football teams.' *Res. Quart.*, **36**.

LANGER, P. (1966) 'Varsity Football Performance.' *Perceptual and Motor Skills*, **23**.

LAYMAN, E. MCCLOY (1960) 'Physical activity as a psychiatric adjunct.' In JOHNSON (ed.) *Science and Medicine of Exercise and Sport*. New York: Harper.

OGILVIE, B. (1968) 'Psychological consistencies within the personality of high level competitors.' *J. Am. Med. Assoc.* Special Report.

OGILVIE, B. and TUTKO, T. (1966) *Problem Athletes and How to Handle Them*. London: Pelham.

OLIVER, J. N. (1958) 'The effects of physical conditioning exercises and activities on the mental characteristics of educationally subnormal boys.' *Br. J. educ. Psych.*, **28**.

SCOTT, J. G. (1960) 'The contribution of physical activity to psychological development in contribution of physical activity to human wellbeing.' *Res. Quart.*, **31**(2), Pt. 2.

SHERRINGTON, SIR CHARLES (1940) *Man on His Nature*. London: Cambridge University Press.

STRAUS, ERWIN (1968) *The Upright Posture*. Symposium of Sports Medicine, University of Kentucky.

VAN DALEN, D. *et al.* (1953) *A World History of Physical Education.* New York: Prentice-Hall.

WARBURTON, F. W. and KANE, J. E. (1967) 'Personality related to sport and physical ability.' In *Readings in Physical Education.* London: Physical Education Association.

WHITING, H. T. A. and STEMBRIDGE, D. (1965) 'Personality and the persistent non-swimmer.' *Res. Quart.*, **36**.

YODER, J. H. (1968) 'The relationship between intellectual and non-intellectual performance. Ph.D. dissertation, Purdue University.

Some aspects of higher level learning processes during adolescence

BARTHOLOMEW, M. (1970) 'Language and judgment levels amongst first- and fourth-year pupils at a county secondary school.' D.C.P. dissertation, University of Birmingham.

BRUNER, J. S., OLVER, R. R. and GREENFIELD, P. M. (1966) *Studies in Cognitive Growth.* New York: Wiley.

DANTO, A. C. (1965) *The Analytical Philosophy of History.* London: Cambridge University Press.

DE SILVA, W. A. (1969) 'Concept formation in adolescence through contextual cues with special reference to history material.' Ph.D. thesis, University of Birmingham.

FLESCH, R. (1950) 'Measuring the level of abstraction.' *J. appl. Psychol.*, **34**(6), 384.

GILLIE, P. J. (1957) 'A simplified formula for measuring abstraction in writing.' *J. appl. Psychol.*, **41**(4), 214.

HALLAM, R. N. (1966) 'Logical thinking in history.' *Educ. Rev.*, **19**.

PEEL, E. A. (1967) 'Some problems in the psychology of history teaching.' In BURSTON, W. H. and THOMPSON, D. *Studies in the Natural Teaching of History.* London: Routledge and Kegan Paul.

PEEL, E. A. (1971) 'Generalising and abstracting.' Letter to *Nature*, **230**, no. 5296, 600, April 30.

RHYS, W. T. (1966) 'The growth of logical thought in the adolescent with reference to the teaching of geography in the secondary school.' M.Ed. thesis, University of Birmingham.

STONES, S. K. (1967) 'Factors influencing the capacity of adolescents to think in abstract terms in the understanding of history.' M.Ed. research, University of Manchester.

WERNER, H. and KAPLAN, E. (1950) 'The acquisition of word meanings: a developmental study.' *Monog. soc. Res. in Child Dev.*, **15**(1).

Intelligence in adulthood and old age

BAYLEY, N. and ODEN, M. H. (1955) 'The maintenance of intellectual ability in gifted adults.' *J. Geront.*, **10**, 91-107.

BELBIN, E. (1958) 'Methods of training older workers.' *Ergonomics*, **1**, 207-221.

BERKOWITZ, B. and GREEN, R. F. (1963) 'Changes in intellect with age.' *J. genet. Psychol.*, **103**, 3-21.

BIRREN, J. E. and BOTWINICK, J. (1957) 'The relation of writing speed to age in the senile psychoses.' *J. consult. Psychol.*, **15**, 243-9.

BIRREN, J. E., BUTLER, R. N., GREENHOUSE, S. W., SOKOLOFF, L. and YARROW, M. R. (eds) (1963) *Human Aging, a biological and behavioral study*. USPHS, NIMH, Bethesda.

BIRREN, J. E. and SPIETH, W. (1962) 'Age, response speed and cardiovascular functions.' *J. Geront.* **17**, 390-1.

BOTWINICK, J. and BIRREN, J. E. (1951) 'Differential decline in the Wechsler Bellevue subtests in the senile psychoses.' *J. Geront.*, **6**, 365-8.

CHOWN, S. M. (1961) 'A factor analysis of the Wesley rigidity inventory; its relationship to age and nonverbal intelligence.' *J. abnorm. soc. Psychol.*, **61**, 491-4.

CHOWN, S. M. (1966) 'The effects of time limits on the assessment of intelligence: a comparison of age groups.' *Proc. 7th Int. Cong. Gerontol.*, Wiener Medizinischen Akademie.

CHOWN, S. M. and DAVIES, A. D. M. (1969) 'Age effects on speed and level in intelligence test performance.' *Proc. 8th Int. Cong. Gerontol.*, Washington.

CORSELLIS, J. A. N. and EVANS, P. E. (1963) 'Observations on the relation of vascular diseases to cerebral degeneration and to mental disorders in old age.' *Social Research Seminar, 6th Int. Cong. Gerontol*, Copenhagen.

DAVIES, A. D. M. (1968) 'Measures of mental deterioration in aging and brain damage.' In CHOWN, S. M. and RIEGEL, K. F. (eds) *Psychological Functioning in the normal aging and senile aged*. Basel: Karger.

FARRIMOND, T. (1961) 'Psychological aspects of the normal decrease of hearing capacity with age.' Unpubl. Ph.D. thesis, Liverpool.

FOULDS, G. A. and RAVEN, J. C. (1948) 'Normal changes in the mental abilities of adults as age advances.' *J. ment. Sci.*, **94**, 133-42.

FURNEAUX, W. D. (1952) 'Some speed error and difficulty relationships within a problem solving situation.' *Nature*, **170**, 37.

GRIEW, S. (1959) 'Complexity of response and time of initiating responses in relation to age.' *Am. J. Psychol.*, **7**(2), 83-8.

HERON, A. and CHOWN, S. M. (1967) *Age and Function*. London: Churchill.

JARVIK, L. F., KALLMAN, F. J. and FALEK, A. (1962) 'Intellectual changes in aged twins.' *J. Geront.*, **17**, 289-94.

JEROME, E. A. (1962) 'Decay of heuristic processes in the aged.' In TIBBITTS, C. and DONAHUE, W. (eds) *Social and Psychological Aspects of Aging*. New York: Columbia Univ. Press.

KENDRICK, D. C., PARBOOSINGH, R. C. and POST, F. (1965) 'A synonym learning test for use with elderly psychiatric patients: a validation study.' *Br. J. soc. clin. Psychol.*, **4**, 63-71.

KLEEMEIER, R. W. (1962) 'Intellectual change in the senium.' *Proc. soc. Stats. section, Amer. Stat. Assoc.*, 290-5.

KRAL, V. A. (1962) 'Senescent forgetfulness, benign and malignant.' *Can. med. Assoc. J.*, **86**, 257.

LIDZ, T. (1970) *The Person.* New York: Basic Books.

LORGE, I. (1936) 'The influence of the test upon the nature of mental decline as a function of age.' *J. educ. Psychol.*, **27**, 100-10.

NISBET, J. D. (1957) 'Intelligence and age; retesting with 24 years interval.' *Br. J. educ. Psychol.*, **27**, 190-8.

NISBET, J. D. and BURNS, R. B. (1965) 'Age and mental ability: retesting with 33 years interval.' *Abstr. Bull., Brit. psychol. Soc.*, **18**(59), 27A.

OBRIST, W. D., KLEEMEIER, R. W., JUSTISS, W. A. and HENRY, C. E. (1963) 'A longitudinal study of EEG-intelligence correlations in old age.' *Proc. 6th Int. Cong. Gerontol.*, Copenhagen.

ORME, J. E. (1957) 'Non-verbal and verbal performance in normal old age, senile dementia and elderly depression.' *J. Geront.*, **12**, 408-13.

OWENS, W. A. (1959) 'Is age kinder to the initially more able?' *J. Geront.*, **14**, 334-7.

OWENS, W. A. (1966) 'Age and mental abilities, a second adult follow-up.' *J. educ. Psychol.*, **51**, 311-25.

RAVEN, J. C. (1938a) *The Mill Hill Vocabulary Scale.* London: Lewis.

RAVEN, J. C. (1938b) *Progressive Matrices.* London: Lewis.

RIEGEL, K. F. (1966) 'A longitudinal analysis of socio-psychological functions.' *Proc. 7th Int. Cong. Gerontol.*, Wiener Medizinischen Akademie.

RIEGEL, K. F., RIEGEL, R. M., and MEYERS, G. (1963) 'The prediction of intellectual development and death: a longitudinal analysis.' *Proc. 6th Int. Cong. Gerontol.*, Copenhagen.

RIEGEL, R. M. and RIEGEL, K. F. (1962) 'A comparison and reinterpretation of factor structure of the W-B, WAIS and HAWIE on aged persons.' *J. consult. Psychol.*, **26**, 31-7.

SEMEONOFF, B. and TRIST, E. (1958) *Diagnostic Performance Tests.* London: Tavistock.

SPIETH, W. (1964) 'Cardiovascular health status, age and psychological performance.' *J. Geront.*, **19**, 277-84.

WEALE, R. A. (1965) 'On the eye.' In WELFORD, A. T. and BIRREN, J. E. (eds) *Behavior, Aging and the Nervous System.* Springfield: Thomas.

WECHSLER, D. (1944) *Measurement of Adult Intelligence.* Baltimore: Williams and Wilkins, 1939 (first edition), 1944 (third edition).

WECHSLER, D. (1958a) *Wechsler Adult Intelligence Scale.* New York: Psychol. Corp.

WECHSLER, D. (1958b) *The Measurement and Appraisal of Adult Intelligence.* Baltimore: Williams and Wilkins.

WETHERICK, N. E. (1965) 'Changing and established concept: a comparison of the ability of young, middle aged and old subjects.' *Gerontologia*, **11**, 82-95.

Colour vision defective art students

ANGELUCCI, A. (1908) 'Les peintures des daltoniens.' *Rec. d'Ophthal.*, **30**, 1-18. Translated by O. Valli and Beauvois.

COBB, S. R. (1972) (Forthcoming paper in *J. Biosoc. Sci.*).

EASTLAKE, C. L. (trans.) (1840) *Goethe's Theory of Colours.* London: John Murray.

GOETHE, J. W. (1894) 'Goethes Naturwissenschaftliche Schriften.' 4 Band, *zur Farbenlehre.* Historischer Thiel II. Weimar: Böhlen.

HEINE, LEOPOLD and LENZ, GEORG (1907) *Über die Farbensehen besonders der Kunstmaler.* Jena: Fischer.

LEIBREICH, R. (1872) 'Turner and Mulready—On the effect of certain faults of vision on painting, with especial reference to their works.' *Not. Proc. Roy. Instn.*, **6**, 450-63.

PICKFORD, R. W. (1951) *Individual Differences in Colour Vision.* London: Routledge and Kegan Paul.

PICKFORD, R. W. (1964) 'A Deuteranomalous artist.' *Br. J. Psychol.*, **55**, 469-476.

PICKFORD, R. W. (1965a) 'The influence of colour vision defects on painting.' *Br. J. Aesthet.*, **5**, 211-26.

PICKFORD, R. W. (1965b) 'Two artists with protan colour vision defects.' *Br. J. Psychol.*, **56**, 421-30.

PICKFORD, R. W. (1967) 'Colour defective students in colleges of art.' *Br. J. Aesthet.*, **7**, 132-6.

PICKFORD, R. W. (1969) 'The frequency of colour vision defectives in a school of art and the influence of their defects.' *J. Biosoc. Sci.*, **I**, 3-13.

PICKFORD, R. W. and LAKOWSKI, R. (1960) 'The Pickford-Nicolson anomaloscope for testing and measuring colour sensitivity and colour blindness and other tests and experiments.' *Br. J. Physiol. Optics*, **17**, 131-50.

PIERCE, W. O'D. (1934) *The Selection of Colour Workers.* London: Pitman.

STREBEL, J. (1933) 'Prolegomena optica zum Bildnerischen Kunstschaffen.' *Klin. Monatsbl. für Augenheilkunde*, **91**, 258-72.

TREVOR-ROPER, P. D. (1959) 'The influence of eye disease on pictorial art.' *Proc. R. Soc. Med. (Ophthal.)*, **52**, 721-44.

WIRTH, ALBERTO (1968) 'Patologia oculare e arti figurative.' *Atti della Fondazione Giorgio Ronchi*, Anno. 23, **4**, Luglio-Agosta, 445-66.

Index